THE HEART
OF
ORTHODOX MYSTERY

The Heart Of Orthodox Mystery

© William Bush, 2003

ISBN 1-928653-12-X

Regina Orthodox Press
PO BOX 5288
Salisbury MA 01952

800 636 2470
Non-USA 978 463 0730
FAX 978 462 5079

www.reginaorthodoxpress.com

TABLE OF CONTENTS

CHAPTER I

The Heart of Orthodox "Lifestyle"

However strongly a non-Orthodox Christian may be drawn by the fullness of Christ he senses to be latent in Orthodoxy, he is, nonetheless, usually startled to discover Orthodoxy's distinctive "lifestyle." Catholics and Protestants alike find this lifestyle excessively demanding when compared with anything they have experienced as Western Christians. After all, few demands are made of a Western Christian when he sits down at the table, save a fairly perfunctory short blessing or, even more convenient, a quick sign of the cross. Then he eats what he wants. Medical restrictions, not religious ones, are normally all that come into play at such a moment.

Ancient Christian tradition, however, weighs heavily upon Orthodox lifestyle. It is the fruit of 2,000 years of focused Christian living, often in a world far more openly hostile to Jesus Christ than is the relatively liberal, generally tolerant society we in North America know today. Nor is this ancient lifestyle limited to Greeks and Russians and other Orthodox of Byzantine culture alone. The so-called "non-Chalcedonian" Orthodox Christians, such as the Copts of Egypt and Ethiopia, not only follow this same lifestyle with a startling strictness, but also esteem it the most basic way to manifest one's seriousness about living as a Christian, just as they tend to judge a Muslim's seriousness about his faith by his keeping of the fast of Ramadan.

The Orthodox Church, aware that she is responsible for proclaiming God as Holy Trinity in a world whose Prince, one must admit, has never been Jesus Christ, matches this fullness of teaching about the Triune God with an equal fullness of Christian culture. Faithfully guarded in Orthodox monasteries from generation to generation, this fullness of culture is often graphically echoed at the table of a practicing Orthodox believer since, to the best of their capabilities and family situations, devout lay people also try to cling to what has been handed down.

1

THE HEART OF ORTHODOX MYSTERY

Being far more aware of unbroken Christian history than most Western Christians, the pious Orthodox believer knows that what has been handed down has been repeatedly confirmed and authenticated in the past by Christianity's most illustrious martyrs, saints and confessors. Without interruption, thousands upon thousands of martyrs, saints and confessors over two millennia have had their personal life in Christ shaped by an Orthodox lifestyle. Moreover, just as intimacy with one's family is rooted in the daily experience of sharing the family table, so too is one's intimacy with the Divine Logos of God, Jesus Christ, also shaped, nurtured and sustained by what takes place at that same family table. Indeed, Orthodoxy aims at deepening a day-by-day, living intimacy with Jesus Christ.

Standing alone in her fundamental insistence that the fullness of God is to be discovered only in the Holy Trinity as revealed by Jesus Christ, Orthodoxy undoubtedly remains more lucid than other forms of Christianity when confronting the world on which He wished to bestow a more abundant life, even emptying Himself of His divine glory in order to become man by the Holy Spirit and the Virgin Mary.

The Orthodox Church is aware of being surrounded not only by non-Christians and non-believers, but also by various heterodox Christians who challenge Orthodoxy's 2,000 years of uninterrupted witness to the holiness of God as Holy Trinity through intimacy with Jesus Christ. An Orthodox lifestyle, moreover, has always provided the indispensable backdrop for this unbroken witness to the way God revealed Himself as Holy Trinity through Jesus Christ. The venerable lifestyle of Orthodoxy, therefore, is worthy of serious respect by any lover of Christ, however off-putting and unfamiliar it may appear at first encounter. Furthermore, the fact that Orthodoxy's lifestyle contrasts so sharply with the lifestyle of most Western Christians should not startle anyone. The ever-changing nature of Western Christianity has never been seen more blatantly or incontrovertibly than it is today, whether in Catholicism or Protestantism.

Since the Council of Vatican II, Roman Catholicism has changed beyond all recognition. Attempts to revive or even preserve the past will continue, but, without a return to Orthodoxy, a general cohesion and consensus will undoubtedly be impossible to attain. As for Protestantism, it has never really ceased to evolve and divide since the beginning of its man-inspired innovations in the early 16th century. Today, liturgically

2

minded Protestants instinctively follow Rome's post-Vatican II lead, as if spiritually still joined to their Western mother by a strand of mystical umbilical chord that was never quite severed at the Reformation. Rome brings her altars out to have the priest face the people, and immediately, by a strange paradox, vast numbers of her more liturgically minded Protestant children blindly follow suit.

For most of the Western faithful, be they Catholics or Protestants, the once-sacred traditions of past generations have, in fact, become so obscured today that they usually appear quite irrelevant, if not downright alien. On the Catholic side, one might cite the weekly abstinence from meat on Fridays, rigorously decreed and widely observed by most Roman Catholics prior to Vatican II. Today, with rare exceptions, it has become a more or less optional practice, often even unheard of by many Catholic young people.

On the Protestant side, one might cite the Anglican Church's abandonment of requiring that the Sacrament of Confirmation be received prior to receiving Holy Communion. Today, in the name of ecumenism, this vestige of Orthodoxy has been swept aside and virtually forgotten in many parishes. Rome actually led the way in this particular assault on sacramental order in the Church of God, unabashedly following that unilateral course she has never ceased to pursue since breaking with her sister Patriarchates of Antioch, Alexandria, Jerusalem and Constantinople in the great schism of 1054. By allowing young children in the 19th century to be given Holy Communion prior to receiving Confirmation, the Pope himself set a precedent for abandoning the time-honored order of Baptism, Confirmation and Holy Communion, common to the undivided Church. Orthodoxy alone maintains that Baptism must be completed by the sacrament of Chrismation prior to the believer's admission to Holy Communion.

ii

Jesus Christ is worshipped in Orthodoxy as the Second Person of the Holy Trinity, the Divine Logos, the only-begotten Son and Word of God. Intimacy with Him, as we have observed, is Orthodoxy's fundamental aim. Ever-conscious of the historical fact that, during the reign of Augustus Caesar, the Second Person of the Holy Trinity took flesh in the person of Jesus Christ by the Holy Spirit and the Virgin Mary, Orthodoxy insists upon joining all aspects of that unique historical event to the life of Orthodox believers as intimately as possible. Indeed, the whole purpose of the Incarnation of Jesus Christ was precisely to make it possible for created man not only to partake of the uncreated and timeless divinity of Christ, but also to join the eternal Godhead of Christ to man's fallen, temporal state.

That Almighty God did indeed walk the face of the earth in the God-Man, Jesus Christ, therefore continually motivates the Orthodox lover of Christ to magnify that historical fact so that it may become the paramount truth by which, for which, and in which he lives. The ideal is for the Incarnation of God in Jesus Christ to become not only the whole basis for his everyday living as an Orthodox Christian, but also the single governing factor of his entire life, the factor to which all else is referred.

Two happenings that occurred during the last week of the earthly life of Jesus Christ are, thus, regularly echoed in the weekly lifestyle of an Orthodox Christian. On Wednesday, one recalls that it was on that day of the week that Jesus Christ, God in the flesh, was basely sold to His enemies, a true Lamb for sacrifice, for 30 pieces of silver by a fellow member of our own human race. On Friday, one recalls that it was on that day that He, God incarnate, was slain by the Romans, accomplishing in His pure flesh and by the pouring out of His precious blood the fulfillment of numerous Jewish prophesies foretelling His Passion and Death. Thus, in the flesh and before men and angels, He actually accomplished in human history that mystical cosmic sacrifice of the Lamb "*slain from the foundation of the world*" (Rev 13:8), as St. John the Theologian termed it, thereby also fulfilling the mystical and eternal purpose of God that lies at the very basis of creation itself.

Remembering man's astounding rejections of Jesus Christ on earth on the Wednesday and Friday of His last week of mortal life, abstinence from meat is decreed by the Orthodox Church for Wednesdays and Fridays throughout the year. Exceptions are allowed only for one pre-Lenten week and for the festive weeks immediately following Easter, Christmas and Pentecost.

The holy fathers teach us rightly that "*the thought of God saves us.*" The Orthodox Church tries, by all means possible, to keep the thought of God ever before her faithful. The dual memory of the Wednesday betrayal and the Friday execution serves this purpose. Throughout his life and as circumstances permit, a practicing Orthodox Christian will at least make an effort to abstain from eating meat on those two days.

The constant memory of God incarnate in Jesus Christ that is promoted by such abstinence cannot but point towards an ever-increasing intimacy with Him. Orthodoxy's most recognizable image, the icon of the most holy Godbirthgiver holding her divine Child, enshrines such intimacy. The great intimacy of the Godbirthgiver with Him is even held up as the intimacy every Orthodox believer should seek and actively pursue. Has not every believer, like her, been called by God to bring Him forth from his own flesh, that men may praise God upon seeing the glory of His divine Son and Logos manifested on earth before men and angels? Is not that glory still manifested to this day in the flesh of Orthodox saints?

Just as we are told that, after the Resurrection, the Apostles always set a place for the Lord Himself at their table, knowing Him to be ever-present with them, so too are the events of that Wednesday and Friday before the Resurrection reflected upon, indirectly if not directly, whenever an Orthodox Christian sits down at the table. He thus becomes aware that the days of his life are indeed significant since they are related to the Incarnation of his Lord, God and Savior, Jesus Christ.

The Orthodox practice of weekly abstinence on Wednesdays and Fridays inevitably leads the outsider into a confrontation with the incalculable role the liturgical calendar plays in Orthodox lifestyle. Though daily commemorations of martyrs, saints and confessors are indicated in the Orthodox *Synaxarion*[1] for every day of the year, the most striking feature of Orthodoxy's liturgical calendar must surely be the Church's unbending fidelity to the Apostolic tradition of glorifying the

---

[1] The multi-volume compilation of the lives of the martyrs, confessors and saints of the Orthodox Church for daily commemorations according to the Orthodox Church year, beginning September 1 and ending August 31.

Resurrection of Christ on the first day of each week of the year. Each Sunday in the Orthodox Church there is a solemn, highly visible, exquisitely articulated commemoration of Christ's Resurrection. Even the casual observer is made aware of the fact that every Sunday is a veritable "little Easter," since the texts sing praise to God for His "great mercy" in delivering the race of men from death and nothingness.

Except on rare occasions, resurrection texts are required to be sung every Sunday. Only on a major feast of the Lord Himself, such as Christmas, is any substitution allowed. On these occasions, the sacred Sunday Resurrection texts can be replaced, for example, by Nativity texts; according to Orthodox liturgical reasoning, these substitutions are, after all, glorifying the birth of Jesus Christ Himself who rose from the dead! However, should even the most solemn feast of the Godbirthgiver and ever-virgin Mary or of any other saint fall on Sunday, a certain number of Sunday Resurrection texts are still required to be sung. Unyielding in her mission to propagate the apostolic teaching of St. Paul that without the Resurrection the preaching of Christ is in vain (I Cor 15:14), the Orthodox Church insists that specific worship of the risen Christ take place every Sunday. It is always a priority that the Lord's Day truly be centered on the risen Christ.

iv

Though somewhat less obvious than the weekly Sunday commemoration of the Resurrection, 20 Sundays falling before and after Easter are blocked off and assigned special commemorations in order to accentuate the centrality of the Easter feast in the Orthodox calendar. These 20 Sundays are comprised of the six Sundays of pre-Lent; the five Sundays of Great Lent; Palm Sunday; and the eight post-Easter Sundays, ending with Pentecost and All Saints' Sunday.

The Orthodox calendar also includes four Lents. The principal one, called "Great Lent," is of course the pre-Easter fast and is familiar, in a somewhat shorter and less rigorous form, to liturgically minded Western Christians. There are also the 40 days of the Christmas fast (November 15 -

December 24), the 14 days of the Virgin's Lent (August 1st - 14) and, finally, the Lent of the Holy Apostles.

Although the Apostles' Lent routinely ends by a particular date (June 29), its start is not predictably triggered by a calendar date like Christmas Lent and the Virgin's Lent. Rather, its placement varies each year with the annual Easter cycle, beginning on the Monday following All Saints' Sunday, the first Sunday after Pentecost. This conjunction of the Easter cycle with the calendar cycle inevitably causes considerable variation in its length each year, since, regardless of the calendar date of its start at the conclusion of the Easter cycle, Apostle's Lent itself is always scheduled to end on June 29. Whatever the varying length may be, what is certain each year is that the Orthodox faithful on the Old Calendar (Julian) will always be keeping the Apostle's Lent for 13 days longer than those on the New Calendar (Gregorian), there being a difference of 13 days between the two calendars.[2]

Orthodox Great Lent begins not on a Wednesday but on a Monday. Greeks call it "Clean Monday," since all non-fasting foods, such as meat and dairy products, are cleaned out of the kitchen as Great Lent's radical shift in dietary habits goes into effect. "Clean Monday" is celebrated in Greece by a public holiday with family picnics of Lenten fasting foods and kite-flying. This light-hearted approach sometimes startles Western Christians, because it sharply contrasts with the "sack-cloth and ashes" approach associated with Ash Wednesday and the rather lugubrious launching of Lent in the West.

For Western Christians uneasy with this seeming light-heartedness on the part of the Greeks, it might be pointed out that one of the West's major spiritual figures after the 1054 schism, the great Teresa of Avila, would undoubtedly have appreciated the Greek's deft gaiety in austerity.

---

[2] Both Old (Julian) and New (Gregorian) Calendarists agree that Christmas is on December 25, and Epiphany on January 6. The Old Calendar, 13 days *behind* the New Calendar, registers the Old Calendar's December 25 as falling on January 7, and its January 6, on January 19. June 29 on the Old Calendar thus falls on the New Calendar's July 12. The subject for disagreement is never the actual *date* on which the feast is celebrated, but rather *which calendar* should be employed in determining that date.

When one of her daughters complained about the austerity of Carmelite life with its long fasts, St. Teresa handed her a tambourine and commanded her to dance: had she not freely and joyously chosen the demanding life of a Carmelite?

Indeed, the Lord's command that we fast in secret with no outward signs sharply contrasts with the West's launching of Lent by smudging ashes on the brows of the faithful on Ash Wednesday. Moreover, though rooted in Orthodoxy's observance of Great Lent, Islam's very public 40-day observance of Ramadan is equally removed from the Lord's admonition to fast in secret.

v

Caught up in the richness and complexity of Orthodoxy's liturgical year, it is easy to neglect, if not actually totally forget, that there is a very basic and highly spiritual challenge lying behind the creation of the Orthodox calendar. This challenge is seldom referred to by those who are born Orthodox and who, at times, live out the calendar's Orthodox lifestyle with a rigor in observing fasting laws that is as startling to the convert as it is edifying. One might well ask if this basic challenge is even an issue for them.

Whatever the case with those born Orthodox, the convert-lover of Christ seeking Christ's fullness in Orthodoxy should never overlook this basic, formidable and all-inclusive challenge, since it involves keeping oneself open to the very heartbeat of the mystery of the Church while struggling with the Orthodox Church's lifestyle. St. Paul's teaching that the Spirit struggles with the letter of the Law elucidates what is at stake: "*for the letter killeth, but the Spirit giveth life*" (II Cor 3:6).

Alas! fervent converts have, on occasion, found their personal fervor for Orthodoxy somewhat dampened by the unrelenting, cyclical demands of fast days and four Lents. Unless naturally inclined towards vegetarianism, they may be dismayed upon discovering that more than half of the Orthodox year's 365 days are, in fact, meatless!

Modern North American society is in no way geared for those who believe in God, even less so for Orthodox Christians who are obliged to

8

remember Jesus Christ every time they sit down at the table; it is, therefore, easy for a new convert's fervor to waver before the impact of demonic powers encouraging him in his despair. He may feel himself lacking in strength and resolution to try to cope with even token observance of the seemingly unrelenting demands of an Orthodox lifestyle. In such a state, he may even be tempted to think that Catholicism or Protestantism no longer look all that unpalatable! Though as a convert he is loathe to admit it, he also knows that, if the truth be told, Western Christianity's lax regard for traditions also attracts many "cradle Orthodox" who may let slip a whispered wish that Orthodoxy would try to "modernize" itself a little bit and modify the rules of the fasts. Even Orthodox bishops may sometimes be heard advocating a "modernization" of the fasting tradition of the Church and even make unilateral pronouncements.

It is at this point that being aware of living within the mystery of the Church may help strengthen the resolution of the lover of Christ to respect the existence of an Orthodox Christian lifestyle, even if his keeping of it is highly imperfect. Through the Holy Spirit, a heightened awareness of the mystery of the Church can serve to protect and sustain the lover of Christ as he pursues his personal vocation of following Christ in Orthodoxy. Within the mystery of the Church, such a vocation is never lived out alone or in total isolation, but in company with all the other suffering, sinful members of the Mystical Body of Jesus Christ, which is the Orthodox Church.

The millions of Orthodox believers who, in spite of their sins, have borne witness for 20 centuries to the value and worth of fasting and praying, just as he, the lover of Christ, is now attempting to do, are indeed his brothers and sisters in Christ. He, a true lover of Christ, must never allow himself to forget all those before him who also loved Christ. Within the mystery of the Church, they are, indeed, forever alive in their prayers raised to Christ, and hence their continuing, abiding presence is available to believers through Christ. The faithful believer is joined to them, because he, too, is a part of that vast and sacred company of struggling, suffering members of the Body of Christ.

Is there a more beautiful or more comforting image expressing the mystery of the Church than that of the most Holy Theotokos extending the protective veil of her all-saving prayers over the whole of the eternally praying Church? This image mystically teaches all Orthodox Christians what it means to cry out to her from the depths of their own sense of isolated solitude, despair and discouragement: *"Most Holy Theotokos, save us!"*

Even so, the consolation of living within the mystery of the Church does not necessarily come naturally to most Western converts. The impact of the West's Renaissance humanism, followed by its even more pernicious and godless man-glorifying Enlightenment, has left most Western Christians with an inordinate sense of self-importance and self-worth quite apart from God. This self-importance and sense of self-worth will inevitably be wounded and visibly offended by the strictly God-centered vision of Holy Orthodoxy.

Undoubtedly, it is this sense of self-importance apart from God that causes Western man to feel himself destined by an unkind God to live and die totally alone in an alien world. Neither Renaissance humanism nor the 18th century Enlightenment emphasized that man must learn to accept his own mystery as a helpless creature, utterly dependent upon God to draw his next breath. And there is certainly no place to be found in all those Western intellectual distortions for the Orthodox sense of the mystery of the Church.

This sense of the mystery of the Church was utterly lacking in the learned monk, Martin Luther, when he made his famous statement, *"Here I stand. I can do nothing else. God help me!"* In contrast, the illiterate Joan of Arc, a century before, in her sublime solitude in challenging the all-powerful theologians of the Sorbonne under the Bishop of Beauvais, proved herself far more aware of the mystery of the Church than Luther. She appealed not just to her own conscience, as did Luther, or even just to the Pope, as a Catholic might be expected to do. She appealed to the whole of the Church, whose representation was woefully inadequate, given that the French tribunal was assembled by the English for the express purpose of burning her as a witch. Looking beyond her own conscience or the Pope, she, unlike Luther, sought justification in the mystery of the whole of the Church of God.

Without even being aware of it, most Western converts to Orthodoxy are, in fact, usually completely fixated on and obsessed by the importance of their own personal conversion to Orthodoxy. "God and me" are all that seem important. This quite common obsession among Western Christians is, of course, reflected in the simplistic question of the fundamentalist Evangelical: "Brother, are you saved?"

The result of such an orientation is that a convert will likely view his life in God as inviolably personal and quite apart from the cosmic mystery of creation itself. Failing to recognize that for an Orthodox Christian the key to the cosmic mystery must always be sought in the Incarnation of Jesus Christ, rather than in the individual himself, he also fails to recognize that he, as a Christian, is inescapably an integral part of that cosmic reality in which he exists and lives from day to day.

To move from the personal and psychological mystery into the cosmic and spiritual mystery of the Mystical Body of Christ -- the Church -- often proves startling, even frightening, to most Western converts. It certainly cannot be denied that even making an attempt to embrace all of creation can only be the fruit of long striving and ever-renewed submission to the Holy Spirit to Whom one repeatedly prays as the "*heavenly King and Comforter*" and the "*Spirit of Truth.*" The wonder, the awe, and the ineffable sweetness of being in harmony with the whole of God's creation by living within the mystery of the Church is, therefore, learned only very slowly and bit by bit through the Holy Spirit by the convert-lover of Christ as he himself is converted into becoming more and more Orthodox.

In truth, all that has gone on for 2,000 years within the mystery of the Church protects an Orthodox Christian. It informs him of just what the Christian life consists. All that has been offered to God in the past has never been lost, either in God or in His Church, beginning with the 144,000 Holy Innocents slaughtered for Christ by Herod's soldiers in the wake of the first Christmas.

This saving heritage is a living, dynamic treasure, amassed over two millennia of Christian history. Within the Holy Spirit alone it is piously guarded and ever vibrant as the basis of the Holy Tradition of the Orthodox Church. All of her children's offerings are part of that vast depository of offerings made through the Holy Spirit to God by members of the human race, stretching back to the beginning of history with the sacrifices of Abel and Noah. This heritage provides the basis for Orthodoxy's maternal concern that each new believer become aware that, in becoming Orthodox, something far more cosmic than just "God and me" is involved.

The Orthodox Christian gradually learns to associate himself with all of this depository of human offerings, both Christian and pre-Christian, which is described with such fidelity and light in the *Synaxarion*. Though it is comprehended fully by God alone and remains largely invisible to man and quite beyond his reach, this precious, mysterious spiritual treasure constitutes, within the depths of the mystery of the Church, a dynamic, living tapestry woven by the Holy Spirit. In it are depicted in a myriad of forms the ever-renewed story of the redemption of sinful mankind, purchased and redeemed by Christ from the fallen world's reign of death and nothingness to which all creation is forever subject outside His almighty and timeless reign.

The Orthodox Church guards the memory of this vast depository of offerings by man to God just as she guards the memory of God's timeless reign, which became a part of her own temporality through Christ's Incarnation. The Orthodox Church does not forget her holy martyrs, whose pain and suffering were freely offered since it was given them, within the divine economy, to be tortured and imprisoned for love of Jesus Christ. In His name they were beaten and their flesh was torn by iron claws. They were flayed alive, devoured by wild beasts, and burned with fire. How movingly St. Paul recalls in his Epistle to the Hebrews those lovers of God who suffered for God even before the coming of Christ into the world.

> *They were stoned, they were sawn asunder, were tempted, were slain with the sword; they wandered about in sheepskins and goatskins, being destitute, afflicted, tormented (of whom the world was not worthy); they wandered in deserts, and in mountains and in dens and caves of the earth.* (Heb 11:37-38).

In addition to all who suffered for God prior to the Incarnation of Jesus Christ, those who still suffer for Him to this day, and those who are yet to suffer for Him (including, perhaps, some who read these lines), there are also those who have experienced the great grace of miracles worked by the loving disciples of Jesus Christ, beginning with the Acts of the Apostles. This is the living, fiery legacy of the saints, which is repeated again and again in the history of the Orthodox Church and remains a daily, tangible reality in an Orthodox country such as Greece.

This joyful glory of God, manifested by His saints and continuing to this day, also constitutes a unique depository of man's experience of God. Through the mystery of the Orthodox Church, it is as readily available to the new convert as it is to the hermit who has spent his life praying alone in the desert. Within that mystery and through the workings of the Holy Spirit, the cosmic fullness of the Incarnation of Jesus Christ, manifested in those who are His, is alive and abundantly present within Orthodoxy for those who seek with pure hearts to be faithful to her Triune God as revealed in Jesus Christ. The Christ-loving convert arriving only during the last hour may, indeed, receive the same pay as one who has worked from the beginning of the first hour. Such is the unbelievable prodigality of the Gospel taught by Jesus Christ.

Therefore, the lover of Christ discovers that he never really prays as a solitary or isolated individual. With God's help, he will gradually begin to sense that he, an humble and unworthy member of the family of the Church, which is made up of millions of members of the Mystical Body of Christ, is actually a personal, living part of the Orthodox Church's prayer for the salvation of the world. In union with all Orthodox Christians who have ever fasted and prayed to God, he too, through his own imperfect attempts at prayer and fasting, strives to bring to God all that he loves, all that with which he struggles, and all that to which he aspires. Additionally, he brings to God all those for whom he prays, both the living and the dead, since within the mystery of the Church there are never limits of time or space. The Orthodox lover of Christ finds himself at one with both the living and the dead, praying far beyond what non-Christians perceive as the normal limits of time and space.

For the convert who has discovered the mystery of the Church, continuous prayer and fasting throughout the year become much more than just an onerous obligation demanded by the Orthodox lifestyle. Regardless of how imperfectly it is done, he comes to view fasting and prayer as a normal part of the Orthodox Church's mighty and ongoing intercession for the whole of creation. This intercession rises to heaven from the four corners of the earth wherever and whenever an Orthodox liturgy is offered to God, with those sublime words proclaiming: "*Thine own, of thine own, we offer unto Thee, on behalf of all, and for all.*" As an Orthodox Christian increasingly comes to grasp the mystery of his participation in this truly universal proclamation, he also comes to understand that it is through the mercy and grace of God alone that the Holy Spirit breathes on him, just as it does on all in Holy Orthodoxy who have been joined along with him to the mystical reign of the Father, Son and Holy Spirit, whether through their own suffering or God's great mercy.

Baptized into Christ and chrismated with the seal of the Holy Spirit, the convert-lover of Christ is led by the Spirit to strive resolutely to his last breath to *become ever more* Orthodox, not only in name and lifestyle, but also in spirit by saying "yes" to the challenge of the mystery of the Church. Thus, the lover of Christ, guided by the Holy Spirit, sets himself upon a road trodden for 2,000 years by every faithful Orthodox believer who, like him, has been called to bear witness to that unspeakable glory of the Father that the Son came into the world to show mankind. That unspeakable glory awaits the true lover of Christ who humbly and prayerfully draws near the Church's mystery with the fear of God, with faith and with love.

CHAPTER II

The Heart of "Putting on Christ" in Baptism

At the very end of an Orthodox baptism, the newly baptized, whom the Orthodox refer to as *"the newly illuminated,"* clothed in white and accompanied by candle-bearing sponsors, follows the priest as they encircle the baptismal font three times, singing a hymn taken from St. Paul's Epistle to the Galatians.

> *As many of you as have been baptized into*
> *Christ, have put on Christ, Alleluia!* (Gal
> 3:27)

The holy Apostle's words provide the final declaration, the definitive statement and, as it were, the last word concerning what has just taken place.

As with everything pertaining to Orthodoxy, Orthodox baptism aims solely at uniting the material with the spiritual; or, in starker, more Orthodox terms, it aims to join the created human being to God, the Uncreated. In baptism, the flesh and blood of created man is being touched by and forever joined to the uncreated, living God in an inexplicable way. The uncreated Creator Himself, by the ineffable power of the Holy Spirit and through the blessed waters of baptism, incorporates man into the Mystical Body of Christ, which is the Church. The newly baptized, having spiritually *"put on Christ"* through baptism, can henceforth find no identity that will not be conditioned by this action of being *"baptized into Christ,"* even should he turn against Christ,

St. Mary of Egypt was a notorious harlot in Alexandria, but she was, nonetheless, a baptized harlot: she had *"put on Christ"* in baptism. Her whole being had been made sensitive to the power of Christ, to whom her sponsors, on her behalf, had once bowed as Lord and God. They had also renounced Satan in her name even though she, prey to inordinate passions of the flesh, had subsequently openly and shamelessly served

Satan and not Christ for many years. Even so, and in spite of all that, nothing could be changed in that she had once and for all *"put on Christ."* The awareness of having *"put on Christ,"* therefore, through the power of the Holy Spirit, did rise up within her in her hour of need, pointing her, the prodigal daughter, back to the Father's house.

When Mary of Egypt found invisible forces preventing her from entering the church of the Holy Sepulcher in Jerusalem to venerate the True Cross of Christ on the September 14 feast of the Exaltation of the Holy Cross, it was as a baptized Christian that she suddenly felt shame at her harlot's life. It was as a baptized Christian that she looked up and saw the icon of the Most Holy Theotokos looking down on her confused state and giving her the grace to pray that the Holy Godbirthgiver would allow her to enter the church and venerate the Cross of the Lord, promising in return a complete change of life. It was as a baptized Christian that she then dwelt in the desert alone, unknown to anyone, with no spiritual guide save the Holy Spirit, for 47 years. She was discovered, through the divine will of God, by the proud Abbot Zossima that he might be humbled by her unusual witness and relay her story, which is as alive and life-giving to Orthodox Christians today as it has been to thousands of lovers of Christ for well over a millennium.

ii

For the person being baptized, Orthodoxy's baptismal texts do imply a lifelong struggle with the challenge of living out the mystery of the Church within oneself. Nor is that struggle totally unrelated to those 47 years of struggle in the desert by Mary of Egypt. Two diametrically opposed and categorical options rise before the newly baptized, even as they also rose before St. Mary of Egypt: the option for a life with God, or the option for a life that excludes God.

When dealing with Christianity, one is dealing not with flesh and blood alone, nor just with human concepts, however noble they may be, whether idealism, philosophy, moral codes or ethical systems. Rather, one is dealing with the living Spirit of the Uncreated God Himself. Christianity's goal is, in fact, far more radical than anything ever achievable by mere idealism or concepts. Through the incessant presence of the Holy Spirit who is "*in all places*" and indeed does fill "*all things*," man's fallen, created state of flesh and blood is to be infiltrated, penetrated and transformed by the "right glory" of the uncreated God who enlightens all who truly "*put on Christ.*"

The lover of God is called, therefore, to sustain the solemnity of his baptismal vows whereby he has "*put on Christ*," whereas He who does not love God may, as often happens, reject the whole lot or, at best, adopt a total indifference to the whole question of the uncreated God in his own affairs. "It's my life, isn't it?" he may ask defiantly and turn away from his baptism.

Such hostile indifference is not at all uncommon. It may even be found among many who, for the sake of men rather than for the sake of God, frequent church services. Though perhaps known as "regular church-goers" they may firmly -- religiously, even -- strive throughout life to keep God "in His place," a place from which, quite obviously, the affection of their own heart is excluded. They are not eager to have any "outside" interference in the living of their lives, believing as they do that they are self-sufficient.

Great numbers of Christians do tend to ignore the profound implications of having "*put on Christ*" in baptism. Without making a sound, they easily and quite naturally sink into a limbo of unchallenged indifference afforded by marginal Christianity. The only challenge they might ever encounter in their entire life in regard to Christianity might well be that of being asked for a baptismal certificate should they marry a spouse whose church requires proof of baptism.

Unfortunately, even for those who are Orthodox, being baptized into the Mystical Body of Christ often means little more than jealously claiming what is seen as one's birthright: membership in a tribal organization providing a sort of spiritual insurance against the tribulations of life. This tribal initiation also opens the door for getting married with tribal rites, as well as being buried according to tribal custom.

What remains utterly removed from the imagination of those having their child baptized in such circumstances is that the baptized child might some day be divinely called to become a martyr or a saint, thereby offering himself in total union with Jesus Christ for the salvation of the human race. For most parents, envisioning such a bizarre vocation as even remotely possible for their newly baptized child is not likely. It is, after all, utterly foreign to "normal life" in the world. How could any "normal" person even conceive of such a possibility? "What does such a vocation have to do with me or my child?" such individuals will probably ask with alarm, viewing the Church as something destined to remain forever totally *outside* themselves, something they are free to take or leave as they are inclined. They cannot begin to imagine that the Church has her own life. They fail to see that the Church is indeed something more than just another humanitarian organization, and they are not really conscious that being baptized really does involve something more than "joining the club." Indeed, the proposition that one has really "*put on Christ*" to become a living part of the Bride of Christ, which is the Church, can really only mean that the mystery of the Church's life thereby forever becomes a part of the mystery of one's own life.

The eternal miracle of the Holy Spirit is continually manifested in Orthodoxy, however, in that throughout 2,000 years of her history, there have always been, from generation to generation, blessed souls who become true lovers of Christ and are highly conscious of having "*put on Christ*" in baptism. Throughout the whole of Christian history, such souls have never failed to emerge in every generation, and they continue to emerge today, providing us with countless saints, martyrs and confessors who illumine the Church of God. They cast upon Him all their humiliations and sufferings, their heartbreaks and destitution. They offer up to Him their setbacks and disappointments even when, as in the case of the Patriarch Job, it seemed that God had taken all from them. As the Holy Apostle wrote, they were "*as having nothing yet possessing all things*" (II Cor 6:10). What does it matter that many of these faithful lovers of God along with the pains of their humble, unsung and lifelong martyrdom, and even their hidden deaths, are forever known only to God? What role have their prayers played in our own salvation?

The extraordinary allegiances demanded and proclaimed at Orthodox baptism -- renunciation of the Devil, followed by bowing to Christ as Lord and King – are, indeed, very strong in their implications. In themselves, they suffice to shape not only the whole direction of the believer's future life in Christ, but also the course of entire cultures and civilizations.

For example, when understood in the depths of its true significance, bowing to Christ, a feature of Orthodox liturgical worship, is in fact an act of free assent to the necessity of living out a whole life within the mystical life of the Mystical Body of Christ, the Church. Indeed, when the newly baptized takes time to reflect upon what was said at his baptism, he will discover that confronting the mystery of the Church is inescapable. Has he not vowed to eternal union with Jesus Christ, the God-Man, the uncreated Logos of the Father? For He, the Logos, the only-begotten Son, together with the Father and the Holy Spirit, reigns in this fallen world by dwelling within the living, beating hearts of those who love Him and call upon His name. To be baptized in His name, therefore, is to make a visible, tangible entry into His mystical Body, the Church, and become a visible witness to the invisible Kingdom -- or Reign -- of the Holy Trinity.

iii

The late Father John Romanides insisted that in speaking of the "*kingdom of the Father, Son and Holy Spirit*," the Greek word translated as "kingdom" would be more accurately conveyed in English by the use of the word "reign." Indeed, the word "reign" does have a distinctly spiritual and mystical dimension that is far more difficult to discern in the word "kingdom." This becomes evident when one associates this kingdom or reign with the holiness which should characterize it. Speaking of a "reign of holiness" seems so much more feasible and less confining that a "kingdom of holiness." The Orthodox Church, moreover, is an outpost of that reign of holiness in this fallen world, encouraging and sustaining all those who, from generation to generation, are called to enter into that kingdom and be sheltered by that reign.

Holiness, however, is by no means something natural to man. Holiness belongs to God alone, even though, in His mercy, God wills that those who love Him be allowed to partake of this uncreated characteristic through the Holy Spirit. Thereby they strive to join themselves to the divine, incarnate Logos, Jesus Christ. Thus, man, by grace, can struggle to become what Jesus Christ is by nature. *"God became man that man might become God,"* the holy Fathers teach us.

However, we repeat, holiness is not a "natural" human characteristic. Wherever and whenever it does manifest itself, observers are usually surprised, if not actually startled. They may even be shocked by the completely unanticipated nature of its manifestations, since it represents an order that is totally and absolutely "other." It does not belong to the fallen, created order according to which man lives in this world, but to an order that is in accord with the will and purpose of the uncreated God.

This uncreated order, necessarily being of a higher nature than the fallen order of the kingdom of this world in which Satan is Prince, inevitably startles us, so settled are we in our earth-bound orientation. The uncreated order forces us to look heavenwards, since we can see around us no earthly reason whatsoever for one to think or act in such an outlandish -- or even scandalous -- way.

Alexis, the Man of God, much venerated by the undivided Church, completely defied all standards for a well-raised young Christian man's "normal" behavior in this world. The son of a Roman senator, Euphimius, Alexis was born after many years of prayer by his sterile parents that they might be given a child. When he reached maturity, they joyously planned his wedding to a highly desirable young woman of their own rank. Alexis, however, desiring above all things to consecrate his virginity to God, took off his new ring on his wedding night and gave it to his bride before disappearing, leaving everything behind: his identity; rank; fortune; and an excellent, but unconsummated marriage.

He fled to distant Mesopotamia where, in the city of Edessa, he was allowed to live for 17 years in the narthex of the church of the Theotokos, clothed in rags as a destitute beggar and supported by alms begged from the faithful. His appearance had changed so radically that servants, dispatched abroad by Euphimius to search for his son and heir throughout the empire, actually gave Alexis alms in Edessa without recognizing him.

At the end of this 17-year period, the Godbirthgiver herself intervened, revealing his holiness to the church's sacristan and ordering him to have "the man of God" leave the narthex and enter into her church. Having been discovered, the saint immediately took flight again. Though he had no intention of returning home to Rome, a storm inadvertently carried his boat there. He accepted this turn of events as divine providence and, in his beggar's rags, returned to his father's house.

Although Euphimius was unable to recognize his son, the terrible loss he and his wife had sustained had softened his heart, rendering him more charitable to others. Without hesitation he ordered his servants to give shelter to the poor beggar for as long as he wished to stay and to feed him with the scraps from his own table. So it was that again, for a period of 17 years, Alexis lived marginally as a beggar, only this time at the very door of his own father's house. He humbly accepted not only his father's charity, but also the insults, mockery and disdain that his father's servants took no trouble to disguise. For them, his presence in no way enhanced the respectable tone of their master's house.

When, at the end of those 17 years, Alexis sensed that his last hour was approaching, he asked for writing materials. Prior to expiring he set down the story of his strange life.

On that very day, Emperor Honorius (384-423) was visiting Rome. A great crowd had assembled in old St. Peter's church for the imperial visit and for the Divine Liturgy that was to be celebrated in the Emperor's presence by the Pope himself. But a voice suddenly coming from behind the altar interrupted the service with a strange order: "*Go find the Man of God: he will pray for the city and for all of you. Even now his soul is leaving his body!*" The faithful had not recovered from their initial shock when the voice spoke again, advising them that the "Man of God" would be found in the house of Euphimius the Senator.

An impressive cortege was formed, with the Emperor and Pope leading. It made its way to the house of Euphimius, where a servant confirmed that for 17 years a beggar, who shared his food with those less fortunate than himself, had been given shelter there by orders of the Senator. The servant escorted them to the beggar's cell where they indeed found his body, a piece of paper clutched in his hand. When read out, the text written by the beggar stupefied everyone. All marveled at how the saint had so patiently and doggedly fought against nature, living at the door of his own father's house as a despised beggar, in order to achieve goods beyond nature.

THE HEART OF ORTHODOX MYSTERY

The weeping, disconsolate parents in their state of shock -- Alexis's mother had long since clad herself in a sack to mourn her loss -- were assured by both the Emperor and the Pope that they had, in fact, given the world a great saint who would reign with Christ for eternity. Moreover, miracles immediately abounded. As the faithful approached the body of the "man of God" the blind saw, the deaf heard, and the dumb opened their mouths to glorify God. The body of the "man of God," which had started giving off a delicious-smelling, healing balm, was thus borne by the Emperor and Pope back to the church to be placed in a jewel-studded golden reliquary.

Such was the way of God. Alexis had been led by the Spirit onto a path that was not of man, but of God, a path that caused the Theotokos in far off Mesopotamia as well as the heavenly voice heard in St. Peter's before the Emperor and Pope to refer to him as "the man of God." Defying all expectations, Alexis had chosen the way of God in preference to the sweetest natural joys legitimately associated with a man of his station and birth.

A more recent, and hardly less scandalous example that God's ways are not like ours was very publicly offered to the world in the latter half of the last century by the late Mother Teresa of Calcutta. When she first began her remarkable work for God, she completely defied the world's way of thinking. She wanted to minister to the dying destitute, whether they were Christians or not, so that each of them would die surrounded by the love of Jesus Christ. Her insistence in applying her idea to persons for whom there was neither hope for recovery nor even for surviving her charity defies all of modern man's scientific reasoning and radically contradicts all common sense. However, Mother Teresa served only the living God, not efficiency, that great god served by the modern world before all other gods. Efficiency experts, of course, could only term her work a totally inefficient waste of effort since it would never produce any on-going, tangible results. Indeed, wasn't the whole operation a wasteful *misuse* of charitable donations?

Be that as it may, Mother Teresa's mission of mercy continued for decades, obliging both her admirers and her critics to confront the mystical, uncreated order of God, however uneasy it made them feel. Just as Alexis, the Man of God, caused his parents and his young bride to confront the uncreated order of God by his quite "unnatural" behavior, so too did Mother Teresa cause the world of her time to face the same mystical reality.

"Nature," in Orthodoxy, is never elevated to a semiautonomous state as it is in Western theology. For the Orthodox, nature ever remains a part of the fallen, created order that can be redeemed by Christ alone. Thus, in Orthodoxy, for example, there is no such thing as "natural grace" as distinguished from "supernatural grace." Nor does God's creation, into which man is born and whose fallen state Christ came to redeem, exist independently and apart from God. In Orthodoxy, "Mother Nature" cannot exist on her own and, as it were, apart from fallen creation.

The breath of the Holy Spirit, who in Christ breathes upon our fallen, created world, constantly recalls us to the uncreated order of God where that "more abundant" life given to the world by Jesus Christ alone is found. New ways of seeing things, such as paying attention to the dying destitute in whom Mother Teresa taught her daughters to see Christ Himself, are brought forth; these are fresh and beautiful things, far beyond man's imaginings. The old, fallen world is challenged by a new freshness of purpose.

iv

The great French Christian poet Charles Baudelaire remarked that God is the unique witness to that drama in which every man is the central character. Indeed, when man's personal drama, out of love for Jesus Christ, is actively offered up to God instead of being regarded as a personal burden or a duty one has a right to bear with resentment, self-pity or ill grace, divine energies are released and made available through the Holy Spirit, just as the dead body of St. Alexis released a sweet-smelling balm and worked miracles of healing immediately after his death. Offered up to God in continuous acts of self-denial, the love of a saint is seen by God in secret ,and we are taught that what God sees in secret, He can reward openly.

So it is that within the glory of the Reign -- or Kingdom -- of the Holy Trinity, the brilliance of all the unknown holy ones of God may well match the brilliance of the glory of known saints. God gives to the last as well as to the first. The hidden sacrifice of some unknown soul -- some crushed mother, for example, who, without bitterness or recriminations, accepts the death of her only child for the love of Jesus Christ -- may well be responsible for unmerited and totally inexplicable graces we are surprised to receive. Perhaps at times we may even wonder why we have been favored with grace that was neither expected nor anticipated but that, we sense, certainly saved us from sudden death.

In the Holy Spirit, the mystery of the Church encompasses the lives of all who seek Christ or who turn towards Him. The Holy Spirit, acting far beyond man's limited conceptual capacities, ever breathes the life-giving breath of creation to bring all to Christ. Through the divine economy, the prayers of some soul far away, and perhaps even totally unknown to us, may have a decisive influence on us. All of that lies within the secret of God, and we will understand it only in the Kingdom. As the holy Apostle wrote: "*Then shall I know even as also I am known*" (2 Cor 13:12) .

Yet the mystery of the Church itself rests upon the mysterious, indefinable action of the divine energies of God being transmitted constantly to us through the prayers of our holy fathers and mothers in Christ. Perhaps nothing is more Orthodox than concluding both public and private worship by praying, "*through the prayers of our holy fathers, O Lord Jesus Christ, have mercy upon us and save us.*"

We may always sense, of course, that all the wondrous rescues from danger we experience in life are the work of God's grace, as indeed they are. But it is the intricate workings of that grace within the divine economy that is the truly awesome mystery that we, because of our sins, are unworthy of understanding. This can never be grasped without the illumination of the divine grace of the Spirit. Yet it is this essential mystery of the Church that, within the divine economy, protects and sustains baptized Christians as they learn to live more intimately in Christ through the Holy Spirit. "*Blessed art thou, O Lord, do Thou teach me thy statues!*" the Orthodox pray, not only when confronting the bodies of their dead, but also Sunday after Sunday before the miracle of the empty tomb of Christ.

St. Nektarios's holy life on earth transpired mostly under the shadow of truly demonic suspicion generated by dark and utterly false accusations launched against him by his fellow-hierarchs in the Patriarchate of Alexandria. Right up until his death in 1920, he was continually opposed and maligned. Today, of course, more than 80 years after his death, St. Nektarios has finally been gloriously vindicated throughout the whole Orthodox world. But today's glorification of the holy Bishop of Pentapolis never consoled him or in any way lessened the utter isolation, deprivation and totally unjust suffering he continually underwent during his lifetime. Even as the saint that he was, he endured this suffering at the hands of the Greek Church's highest hierarchs in Alexandria and Constantinople, who not only rejected him, but also scorned him as a marginal, outcast bishop with a suspect past.

Be that as it may, on the island of Aegina, solidly perched on the hillside just below St. Nektarios's modest Holy Trinity women's monastery, we see rising today what is purported to be the largest Orthodox Church in all of the Balkans. It has been raised not by the hierarchs, but by the Orthodox faithful themselves, as if the reply of the Holy Spirit Himself, working through the people of God, to those powerful hierarchs who scorned the suffering witness of the maligned Bishop of Pentapolis. Like St. Alexis, St. Nektarios was truly a "man of God." His strange, marginal life appears as concrete and highly tangible proof of the power of God to stoop to those who love Him above all things, regardless of what the Orthodox hierarchs of his time said about him.

Thousands upon thousands of God-loving pilgrims from all over the Orthodox world flock to Aegina today seeking the blessing of this "man of God" who was so shabbily treated by the officials of the Greek Orthodox Church of his time, and yet is still so potently with us in Jesus Christ. Within the divine economy, is it not possible that the truly miraculous rebirth of Greek monasticism that began in 1970, exactly 50 years after St. Nektarios's death, is related to his unceasing and lifelong intercession for a vibrant monastic life in Greece? Moreover, would not the holy intercession of St. Nektarios still arise today before the face of God, protecting the expansion of Greek monasticism outside Greece and even in America?

The astounding manifestation of how God works in saints such as St. Nektarios continues to demonstrate how God, who sees in secret, sometimes does reward quite openly those who love Him above all things. It is they whom He has called to show forth His glory, thereby totally confounding their ecclesiastical enemies. With the most holy Godbirthgiver and with all the Church, they too join in singing joyously at the end of Matins: "*He hath put down the mighty from their seat and hath exalted the humble and meek*" (Lk 1:52). Such is the constant refrain of those chosen holy ones of God who bring forth Christ from their own flesh as St. Nektarios did.

v

Being baptized into the Mystical Body of Christ is, therefore, something quite different from just becoming a member of an organization such as a club, a lodge, or any other similarly human group. Those who are members of the Mystical Body of Christ become witnesses to the Uncreated God through their participation in the Church's mystical nature, a nature communicable to the faithful through their prayers and their participation in the Mysteries -- or Sacraments -- of the Church. The witness they bear, moreover, is not a witness to the greatness of human courage and fortitude, but rather to the power of God alone to transform nature. For it is the power of the Holy Spirit, and not the power of man, that takes fallen human nature and transfigures it, redeeming it in Christ.

Daily invoking the Holy Spirit, Orthodox Christians know through experience that man's fallen nature is changed only gradually as one struggles to respond to the Spirit poured out on it, freely "*in all places and filling all things.*" Through the power of God, man can become enlightened, transformed, and made new. He can, of course, even be transfigured in the blink of an eye, as it was with St. Paul on the road to Damascus. Yet that image of immediate conversion is further removed from our experience than the images we have of that great Apostle to the Gentiles and author of half the New Testament struggling and suffering for the churches of God for many years before finally achieving the crown of a martyr's death.

Fallen man, created in the image and likeness of God, within the mystery of the Church, and by the mystery of his own baptism, is always being inwardly pulled and tugged towards something far beyond what is merely human. Yet fallen man's human nature is never violated. He is

26

ever free. As holy as a saint may become, he is a saint because he is, for all eternity, a fallen sinner who strove to use his God-given freedom to allow himself to be redeemed by God in Christ, through the Holy Spirit. Saints are never saints because they are granted a special, privileged status by God, automatically elevating them above the trials, sorrows and struggles every baptized soul must contend with.

Yet some saints' bodies, like that of St. Alexis or, more recently, that of St. Nektarios, do sometimes stream with sweet-smelling myrrh and work miracles. Indeed, the holy ones of God do sometimes manifest the power of God working through them in all sorts of ways, such as appearing to certain chosen ones to guide, instruct or heal them or, as in the case of St. Nektarios, to see his prayers for the revival of Greek monasticism bear such glorious fruit 50 years after his death. All of these things are possible with God through the Holy Spirit, *"for when God wills, the order of nature is overcome,"* as we sing in regard to the birth of Christ by the Most Holy Godbirthgiver.

Saints and the wondrous manifestation we experience from their witness are, in fact, a part of that living, dynamic and ongoing mystery that is the Church of God. All of this is a part of the plentitude of power and presence of the all-conquering Christ that is being fused into the life of all those who have *"put on Christ"* in baptism. This is always dependent, however, on the extent to which they feel called to love Him and humbly seek to serve Him, and Him alone. The Orthodox Church knows that whoever prayerfully and longingly entreats the *"Heavenly King and Comforter"* to *"come and abide"* in him is actually opening himself deliberately to the power of the Christian God, the Holy Trinity, the uncreated Creator of heaven and earth and of all things visible and invisible.

The Orthodox Church never tires of recalling the dynamic existence of this vast, mystical fellowship where all who have belonged to Christ are joined together in witness to proclaim in heaven, as on earth, not only that God exists, but that His glory is to be found in all its fullness within the mystery of the Church. Indeed, the Orthodox vision of *"every righteous soul, made perfect in faith, who, since the beginning of time has pleased God,"* stretches the horizon of the Orthodox consciousness towards the eternal realities of heaven, far surpassing the brief, passing temporalities of life on this fallen planet.

Because of the mystical nature of her very structure, encompassing both the temporal life of her members living in this world and the eternal life of all those righteous souls who have gone before us and dwell in God, one may say that the Orthodox Church's heartbeat is, in fact, the authentic continuation of that heartbeat of faith and witness by which man has sought communion with his Creator from the beginning of time. It was within the divine economy, through the mercy of our man-loving God, and out of man's need for more intimate communication with His Creator that, "*in the fullness of time*" (Ep 1:10), God was incarnate in Jesus Christ and revealed Himself as Holy Trinity and the friend of man. It is into this fellowship of intimacy with the Triune God that one is baptized and truly "*puts on Christ.*" It is the realization of that intimacy in his life that remains the lifelong challenge of the Orthodox Christian.

CHAPTER III

The Heart of Being "Living Epistles"

In her role as God-appointed intercessor for the race of man, the Orthodox Church prays ceaselessly for the whole world. The most basic daily challenge confronting a member of the Orthodox Church, therefore, must be that of learning to consent, through the Holy Spirit, to active and personal participation in the mystery of the Church's cosmic prayer. Moreover, as is generally true whenever one is dealing with the affairs of God, this act of consent must be reaffirmed repeatedly, again and again, day by day, and even minute by minute. Indeed, at the heart of Orthodox spirituality lies the personal practice of the "Jesus Prayer," whereby one strives to pray, with every breath, "*Lord Jesus Christ, Son of God, have mercy upon me a sinner.*"

It is only within the mystery of the Church that the lover of Christ gradually comes to realize that, from the beginning of time, he has forever been a small part of the whole of creation, and that he is thereby inextricably and ineluctably related both to God and to all of God's creation. Through the mystery of the Church he begins to grasp, bit by bit, that all that he does mystically affects not just himself, but, in union with Christ and within the divine economy, the whole of the Church's cosmic witness for God in the fallen world. In the *Canon of the Harrowing of Hell*, sung both on Good Friday and at Holy Pascha, the Orthodox sing "*Though in Adam my person was hid, it was not hidden from Thee, O thou Lover of mankind,*" signifying the inestimable role potentially granted each human soul. Though hidden from the beginning of time in Adam, it has always been perceptible to the omniscient, all-seeing eye of the Word-Creator-Redeemer of the world, Jesus Christ, the All-Powerful, Who is the Lamb of God slain from the foundation of the world.

Salvation has, in truth, been offered to the world because the Second Person of the Holy Trinity emptied Himself of His glory in order to be made man through the Holy Spirit and the Virgin Mary. He came down from heaven to be incarnate in Jesus Christ. In response, all His followers are continually being called upon to empty themselves of all that is not the Lord Himself, that He may become all in all for them. Furthermore, He has willed that it be through them and their loving offerings to Him that He continue to be made manifest in the world. Through the Holy Spirit, their witness, showing Him at work in themselves, enlightens others that they too may confess the glory of Jesus Christ as Lord to the glory of God the Father.

Holy Orthodoxy patiently seeks to wrest man from his self-sufficient solitude, teaching him complete confidence in his utter dependence upon the Triune God. Attaining this utter dependence upon the Triune God is by no means something unique to the individual alone. It is a common characteristic shared by all who have loved God throughout the history of creation. Within the mystery of the Church, moreover, the lover of Christ can, through the Holy Spirit, actually be mystically joined to this *"cloud of witnesses"* (Heb 12:1) as he turns himself increasingly to God and learns to discover this sublime and ineffable fellowship of which he is now a part.

Orthodoxy, being the fullness of Christ, profoundly increases man's sense of needing to refer to God in absolutely everything, for sanctity is not just the final goal, but actually the only means of attaining that goal. There is then, for the lover of Christ, if he accepts the challenge of living within the mystery of the Church, no alternative either to absolute and utter dependence upon God or to total submission to His divine wisdom.

Indeed, it cannot be repeated too often that, through the Holy Spirit, one becomes holy only by the struggle to become holy. Within the divine economy by which, with which, and in which we are all given to pray within the mystery of the Church, the Triune God wills to take up His abode in the lover of Christ. Within the lover of Christ, the Holy Spirit Himself confesses the lordship of Christ to the glory of God the Father. This divine action, rooted in the dynamism of the uncreated life of God within the Holy Trinity, occurs concretely every time the believer humbly prays with a pure heart, *"Lord Jesus Christ, Son of God, have mercy upon me a sinner,"* since St. Paul teaches that *"no man can say that Jesus is the Lord, but by the Holy Ghost"* (I Cor 12:3).

Each repetition of the Jesus prayer is, therefore, a confession by the Holy Spirit that Jesus Christ is Lord, a confession impossible to man without the aid of the Holy Spirit. Thus, in him who prays, "*Lord Jesus Christ, Son of God, have mercy upon me a sinner,*" there is a movement of the great love, the great light, and the great power of the Holy Trinity itself taking place, since, within the heart of the person praying, the Holy Spirit is indeed confessing within him the Lordship of Christ to the glory of the Father. The constant repetition of this confession of the Holy Spirit cannot but serve to draw the one who is praying, so long as his heart is pure and free of passions, into more and more intimate communion with the Triune God at work within him.

ii

The fulfillment of God's creation, as understood by Christians, is centered in the workings of the Mystical Body of Christ itself. It is a fulfillment that is, in fact, constantly being repeated and continually being carried out within each individual praying member of the Body of Christ. Its scope is thereby always being renewed. Thus, the action of the Holy Spirit within the Body of Christ is both expressed as well as expounded through the unique witness of each believer, however humble it may be.

The calling of one member is never quite identical to the calling of another. Indeed, since the beginning of creation, within the divine economy, each individual has received a calling unique to himself, be it Abel, Enoch, Noah or Abraham, Moses or Elijah. Thus, we may affirm that no one prophet, no single witness for God can ever be replaced by another witness or another prophet. One of the givens of God's creation is that no image of God is ever identical to any other. Within the divine economy, each image of God is utterly unique. This very basic truth concerning God's creation never needs to be explained to a mother in regard to her own child, for she knows that one child can never replace another. After all, even a cloned child would still have its own unique experiences, its own needs, and its own reactions.

The demonic, which is forever impotent to create and is jealous of the uniqueness of all these individual images of God, works diligently to obscure man's sight in perceiving this uniqueness. It is always the Enemy who leads men to say dismissively, "a drunk is a drunk" or "a whore is a whore," since inveterate sin does seem outwardly to reduce man to a particular type once he renounces striving to transform his fallen nature into the completely unique image of God it was created to be. A notable example exists in the case of St. Mary of Egypt: some scornful Christian observer might well have remarked, as he saw her seeking clients among the pilgrims on the boat from Alexandria to Jerusalem, "a whore is a whore."

Thus, while one may tend to think that one monk must be like another monk or one nun like another nun, and to such an extent that they really would be interchangeable, they are not, in fact, any more interchangeable as individuals than are any two children or any two parents or grandparents. God has willed that man be created in His image, yet, even so, each image is a unique mystery, distinct from all others. God's glory manifested by one saint will never be identical to the glory manifested by another saint. Though there is but one glory of God, each saint's transmission of it is unique.

The prayer of every Orthodox Christian will, thus, be shaped by the God-given mystery of the person praying, however small a part of the Church he represents. Each of these unique prayers rises to God, moreover, within the mystery of the Church. The prayer of a Patriarch or Pope is of no greater merit before God than is the prayer of a crushed child or a wretched beggar whose prayer rises from his heart. All true prayer rises before the face of God as the prayer of fallen creation beseeching its Creator. He alone can weigh and measure the extent to which His creatures truly pray with love and pure hearts within the Holy Spirit, be they beggars, priests, bishops, popes, or patriarchs.

Thus, the Church of God, through the Holy Spirit, does offer up, in union with Christ, every member of His suffering Body, the Church, as a completely unique and irreplaceable offering before men and angels. The implication of the necessity for each individual member of the Body of Christ actually to become a living sacrifice and to offer himself up before men and angels can only serve, through the Holy Spirit, to unite both the lover of Christ and the witness he bears to those countless other witnesses of sacrifice and heroic courage demonstrated by the God-bearing martyrs throughout the Orthodox Church's long unbroken history. Each believer thus becomes a part of that "*so great a cloud of witnesses*" *(Heb* 12:1) of which St. Paul speaks, surrounding us and incorporating not just the known Christian saints, but all who, since the beginning of time, have glorified God, the Creator and Preserver of all things.

iii

The philanthropic God sung by Orthodox Christianity has indeed willed that His holiness be manifested in those who love Him, so that men may see His glory and raise their hearts and souls to Him. Man, who before the Incarnation of the Second Person of the Holy Trinity in Jesus Christ had no offering to give God other than the sacrifice of the blood of animals and the fruits of the earth, was given, in the Incarnation, a unique offering in which God offered Himself for man as a man, Jesus Christ, in a cosmic sacrifice, an offering made once and for all. Through man's memory, and in the Holy Spirit, this offering is eternally present and available to the lover of Christ. Until the end of time, man is free to draw continually upon its all-saving power. Those who have experienced repeatedly plunging themselves into this unique offering of Jesus Christ know that not only is each man renewed through the offering of Christ, but all creation around him is also renewed.

At every Divine Liturgy, therefore, the cosmic sacrifice of the divine Logos of God, once offered on Calvary, is once again entered into mystically by those standing before God in their parish church on earth, as well as by the saints and angels who stand before God in heaven. It is, therefore, but a natural reaction that some of the faithful may be moved to fall to their knees when the words, "*Thine own, of thine own, we offer unto thee, on behalf of all, and for all,*" are proclaimed by the sacrificing priest over the holy sacrifice just offered: therein resides the very heart of the mystery of the Church.

The Church exists neither as a sort of spiritual clearinghouse nor as some sort of super prayer-agency whose purpose it is to broker man's offering to God. Rather, the Church exists to allow man, with all his body, mind and soul, to participate mystically in nothing less than the unique offering of Christ Himself. For it is Jesus Christ Himself to Whom the liturgical text refers in those initial words "*Thine own, of thine own.*" It is

33

Him whom we boldly offer up to God at every Divine Liturgy "*on behalf of all, and for all.*" It is because, in our poverty, we have nothing else to offer, for we always stand before God at each Sunday's Liturgy naked and bereft of any merit or worth.

However, the extent to which we ourselves are united to Him and actually live in Him, and He in us, is the extent to which we are also a tiny part of that first cry of "thine own." This is not because of who we are, but because of what He, within the mystery of the divine economy, is to creation itself. United to Him, we too are offered up with Him, Jesus Christ, who indeed is being referred to in the first cry of "thine own."

At this most solemn moment of the Divine Liturgy, as the proclamation "*Thine own, of thine own, we offer unto Thee, on behalf of all, and for all*" resounds, all faithful lovers of Christ can only seek their salvation in Him who is of God, who both offers Himself and is offered up to God as the incarnate Logos and only-begotten Son. The Lord's petition, "*that they all may be one; as thou, Father, art in me and I in thee, that they may all be one in us: that the world may believe that thou hast sent me*" (Jn 17:21), is thereby fulfilled. Indeed, one may say that the high priestly prayer of the Lord on the evening before His sacrifice is actually mystically answered every time the Divine Liturgy is offered, joined as it is with the prayers of those, living and dead, who unite themselves to Him and to His sacrifice.

How great is God's mercy and glory bestowed upon us mortal men! We are empowered to offer up to Him none other than His own Self as victim of sacrifice while, at the same time, as "little Christs," to be mystically joined to Him in this sacrifice as actual members of His Body! How meet it would be not only that the whole congregation be kneeling at that point, but actually prostrate, with their faces to the floor, before the Lord of heaven and earth to Whom, in that moment, by His great mercy, their whole lives are united as they join themselves to His unique sacrifice made once and for all on Calvary.

Assuming the full implication of these words raises basic questions, of course. Do we really want to exist only in Christ, something impossible without the Holy Spirit's sustenance? Is such a "radical" orientation of our life what we really desire? Or, if the truth be told, would we not really prefer to hold back in giving an unconditional "yes" to the divine life offered us at every minute of every day, once we are baptized into Christ?

The selfless disposition of wishing to live only in Christ, conforming our life to the eternal and divine life we find only in Him through the Holy Spirit, is, of course, learned fully only by the great saints. Yet, through God's great mercy, it is possible for seemingly ordinary men to be touched by the Spirit of God and suddenly grasp the vanity of all that is not God and, by that realization, desire to become holy. This is a great grace. Such a man, by the Holy Spirit, has thus truly been freed to enter into Christ fully, to abide in Christ, and to allow Christ to take up His abode in him.

So it is that repentant sinners such as our holy Mother, St. Mary of Egypt, become vibrant parts of that universal cry of Orthodoxy: "*Thine own, of thine own, we offer unto thee, on behalf of all, and for all.*" Their sins, regardless of the greatness of their magnitude, no longer mattered, for, through the Holy Spirit, Christ came to dwell in them, taking up His abode in them as He became all in all for them. By the Holy Spirit they were transformed by the power of Christ. Even today the divine energies continue to stream forth from them as saints, illumining, through the Holy Spirit, all those who honor and love them within the mystery of the Church.

iv

To converts in Corinth, St. Paul wrote that they themselves, being of flesh and blood, were now "*manifestly declared to be the epistle of Christ*" (II Cor 3: 3), that is, the living, *visible* witnesses of Christ Himself. As an "*epistle of Christ,*" moreover, they were not written "*with ink,*" but rather "*with the Spirit of the living God.*" Indeed, that "*epistle of Christ*" that they themselves were, St. Paul writes, is written "*in fleshly tables of the heart,*" quite unlike the Law of the Old Testament, written on tables of stone. This is because St. Paul and his helpers, by God's will, had been made "*ministers of the new testament, not of the letter, but of the spirit, for the letter killeth, but the spirit giveth life*" (II Cor 3: 6).

St. Paul, the converted Pharisee, insists that the glory of the New Testament of Christ is far more glorious than the glory of the Old

Testament. Fusing the Lord Jesus Christ to this ministry of the Spirit he is now called to carry out, the Apostle contrasts its glory with the now-surpassed glory of the Old Law, which, within the limits of the Old Testament, could only deal with man's condemnation. He therefore asks: *"How shall not the ministration of the spirit be rather glorious? For if the ministration of condemnation be glory, much more doth the ministration of righteousness exceed glory"* (II Cor 3: 8-9). The glory of God was indeed manifest under the Law, but that glory -- the glory of Sinai, for example -- has now been far surpassed by the glory of the risen Christ, be it the glory of the Resurrection itself or that same uncreated glory manifested by Christ on Mount Tabor at the Transfiguration.

St. Paul finishes off this passage with this observation regarding the glory pouring forth from Christ: *"But we all, with open face beholding as in a glass the glory of the Lord, are changed into the same image from glory to glory, even as by the Spirit of the Lord"* (II Cor 3:18). For the lover of Christ, having found the fullness of Christ in Orthodoxy, does indeed become, like St. Paul's converts in Corinth, a part of that living epistle written on the fleshly tables of hearts bearing witness to the Spirit of Christ. Indeed, the Holy Spirit Himself, who is truly *"the Spirit of the Lord"* (II Cor 3:17), frees the lover of Christ from all the legalistic constraints of the letter of the law since *"where the Spirit of the Lord is, there is liberty"* (II Cor 3:17). And in this wondrous liberty granted by the Spirit of the Lord, the lover of Christ, beholding as in a mirror the glory of the Lord, is *"changed into the same image from glory to glory, even as by the Spirit of the Lord"* (II Cor 23:18).

One cannot guarantee, however, that the lover of Christ who embraces just the laws and regulations of the Orthodox Church -- that is, the "lifestyle" -- will thereby automatically partake of the "right glory," alas! The "right glory" of trying to live out the laws and regulations of one's Orthodox life can come only when it is attempted through the Spirit of God Himself. "Right glory" is never automatic, but always dependent upon man's inmost freedom to say "yes" to God.

The mystery of the Church, the ineffable movement of the Holy Spirit within the Church, can never be pinned down, for it is neither mechanical nor scientific, being vivified by the Holy Spirit Himself who is the "Giver of Life." The late Elder Paisios (+1994) observed that Christians climb to heaven without mechanical means. This is true because one must ever rely on the movement of the Spirit, which can never be programmed.

For 2,000 years this mystery of the Church has defied all description, and it shall continue to defy it. Freely entered into through the consenting heart of the believer, the mystery invisibly and wondrously sustains the Orthodox Church in her sorrowing, imperfect history of witness to the kingdom -- or reign -- of the Holy Trinity. As was demonstrated at the crucifixion of the Lord, man's heart, as was the case with the "bad" thief, may either be closed to the Spirit through man's arrogance, anger and bitterness, or it may be opened to the reign of Christ through the Spirit, as it was in the case of the "good" thief. To him the Lord said that he would, that very day, be with Him in Paradise.

Trying to be an Orthodox Christian while refusing to open oneself to the great mystery encompassing the Orthodox Church's incredible existence and cosmic witness in the world might well be likened to trying to live by the letter of the law, Old Testament style. It is only as a free son of the Spirit of God that one bears witness to the mystery of the Church, manifesting the "right glory."

v

Quite wrongly, Orthodoxy itself is sometimes looked upon as a religion of the law, or of laws. It is usually presented as such by Orthodox zealots who are eager to push aside God's creation in favor of their illusions about an idealized creation of their own making. In such a creation, their minds can envisage the Church as they think it should be but, taking into account the state of fallen creation, never is, or never can be. The Papacy, with its enforced celibacy of the clergy, is a perfect example of such idealization, as is the Protestants' desperate attempt to realize their obsession with an imaginary primitive church "purity" that never existed. Even today's unraveling of the very fabric of Western Christianity is not divorced from idealization that, being demonic, is as present with the Orthodox zealots as with the most liberal Protestant. All these merely human attempts to approach the Church are the fruit of man's idolatrous idealization of the Church.

The only goal for which Orthodox Christians should strive is that of learning to accept the ongoing role of being very humble partakers of the Church's divine mystery. Though they are weighed down by the history and the untold sins and failings of Orthodox Christians of the past and present, they still possess, by divine grace alone and not their own merits, the ineffable heritage of two millennia of martyrs, saints and confessors who have uninterruptedly proclaimed Orthodoxy's basic faith in the Holy Trinity as revealed in Jesus Christ Who Himself is both God and Man.

This is nowhere better exemplified than in the definition one gives of the word "Orthodox." According to SS. Cyril and Methodios, Orthodox means "right glory," the two words used by them for translating the Greek word "Orthodox" into Slavonic. Modern Greeks, having forgotten even the possibility for the word to have meant, a thousand years ago, anything other than today's modern definition as "right teaching," "right doctrine" or "right worship," tend to insist that such a translation has nothing whatsoever to do with them, the Greek language, or even Orthodoxy itself.

Non-Greeks can only wonder why most Greeks today refuse this truly holy translation made by learned and holy Greek saints a thousand years ago, a translation destined to shape the glorious witness for God made by Slavic Orthodoxy from the beginning. The emphasis with which "right glory" is rejected by many Greeks as a proper translation for the word "Orthodox," whether by sophisticated argument or arrogant indifference, as if the question had absolutely nothing whatsoever to do with them, can only rouse one's suspicion that there is, indeed, a spiritual factor involved. Denying "right glory" as the true translation of "Orthodox" does oppose the most spiritually luminous interpretation possible of Orthodoxy for an English-speaker. Moreover, with "right glory" having been set up as the foundation stone of Slavic Orthodoxy from the beginning, what Greek can deny that the Slavs have shown forth the "right glory" in their saints, and that that "right glory" is the same "right glory" always discernable in Greek saints? Paradoxically, however, modern Greeks are shy about naming it "right glory."

The love today's Greeks show, for example, for the holy Russian peasant St. Silouan the Athonite (+1936) or for St. Seraphim of Sarov would tend to confirm that they too recognize the "right glory" of the Slavs as being their own Orthodoxy. As a striking example, one might also cite the devotion that Elder Amilianos of Simonas Petras and his spiritual daughters at Ormylia Monastery bear the Russian St. Herman of Alaska, whose relic they venerate with such devotion. Does not their love for this Russian-American saint bear witness to the truth that there is but one glory in the Lord, and that that glory -- who can dispute it? -- is, indeed, the "right glory" of the holy Orthodox faith? That most Greeks today refuse to accept what was not only accepted, but actually put forward in the early 10th century by Saints Cyril and Methodios as the true meaning of "Orthodox" - that is, "right glory" - when it was translated into Slavonic calls for serious reflection on the spiritual implications of such a refusal.

Indeed, this definition of "Orthodox" is much more than a question of semantics. The definition of "orthodox" usually accepted by the anti-"right glory" Greeks is either "right teaching," "right doctrine" or "right worship," all of which imply a purely intellectual dimension. "Right glory," however, places the debate on a much higher level, since "right glory" is far beyond the merely intellectual. "Right glory" points us to a *spiritual*, a *mystical* dimension involving that glory actually becoming a part of our own person, bearing witness to the Light of Christ burning in us. According to His great high priestly prayer in the 17th chapter of St. John's Gospel, was not the purpose of the Lord's coming into the world precisely that the Father might glorify Him? He prays, "*with thine own self with the glory which I had with thee before the world was*" (Jn 17:5) so that men might see and experience the "*glory which thou hast given me*" (Jn 17:24).

The Greek word for "glory" used throughout St. John's Gospel is "doxa," universally translated into English as "glory." Is not "heterodox" normally translated as "other glory"? Of course, one can hardly expect English dictionaries to pick up on the Slavonic translation for "Orthodox," that is, "right glory," since "right glory" is a purely mystical and spiritual translation -- a uniquely Orthodox Christian translation -- implying the divine action of the Holy Spirit at work in man to make manifest the divine glory found in Holy Orthodoxy alone.

This glory of Jesus Christ as perfect God and perfect man has, moreover, revealed God to us as three persons in one God, "*Father, Son and Holy Spirit, the Trinity, one in essence and undivided,*" as we sing at the Divine Liturgy. This "right glory" raises man to the level at which the Holy Trinity itself is at work in the world, far beyond man's intellectual activities or limitations, for it is the Holy Spirit within the mystery of the Church Who motivates all things.

"Right glory," therefore, demands a great deal more from the believer than the merely intellectual assent demanded both by "right doctrine" and "right teaching." One may consent to anything intellectually without actually manifesting the "right glory" within oneself. The Spirit does manifest the living presence of God in man by the "right glory" seen in him. It is this, of course, that continues to threaten the power of the Enemy of the human race, since the Evil One wills that the Church of God forget even the words "right glory," which so accurately and faithfully keep this idea alive.

"Right worship," though much nearer to the basic dynamism of Orthodoxy's claims for every convert, still is far less precise than "right glory" in accurately defining what Orthodoxy is all about. There is, indeed, something special and very particular about an Orthodox Christian who is full of "right glory," distinguishing him not only as being distinctly Orthodox in his belief and way of worship, but also as someone with some obvious experience of God. It is not for nothing that both Protestants and Catholics are referred to as "heterodox." They are of "another glory" that is not the "right glory" of holy Orthodoxy.

A "right glory" Christian seeks the right glory of his Christian God and clings to it in such a way that no one in an Orthodox congregation is astonished, curious, upset or uncomfortable to see the tears of a "right glory" Christian flow while standing silently in prayer before God in church. Nor is anyone disturbed if a "right glory" Christian should quietly stand holding a candle or make a prostration, face down on the floor, for reasons known only to himself and to God. Freedom from conformity and from all concern of what others might think seem to characterize "right glory" Christian behavior when worshiping God in the Orthodox Church.

I once saw a "right glory" Russian lady, the wife of a distinguished theologian in Paris, quietly fall behind an ecumenical group of Christian pilgrims in England to prostrate herself before the tomb of every saint of the undivided Church buried at Canterbury, kissing each tomb with multiple signs of the cross. On the night of holy Pascha, after the long Pascal Liturgy, which was celebrated by the Greeks at our local exhibition grounds since the parish church was far too small to accommodate all the worshippers, I once offered a ride to a "right glory" Greek woman who was carrying a lantern lighted with the holy fire of Easter. She, however, refused both my offer and all other offers for a ride home, even though it was miles, not blocks, that she had to cover on foot, and hours rather than minutes that her return home would take. Full of the "right glory," she had promised God that she would return on foot, announcing the Resurrection of Christ to every house she passed between the exhibition grounds and her home. Unworthy to behold such glory, I humbly and prayerfully watched as she disappeared down the street at two o'clock in morning, bearing witness to the "right glory" of Holy Pascha along the main street of London, Ontario, swinging her lantern in the direction of every house she passed with Orthodoxy's cosmic cry of Easter on her lips: "Christ is risen! Christ is risen!"

In my student days in Paris, I recall a "right glory" Old-Calendarist Greek widow whose minuscule squat, black form was rendered unforgettable by the great light that ever blazed in her gaze when she came, as a regular worshipper, to St. Sergius's Theological Institute to pray. Since the seminary's distinguished scholar-rector, Bishop Cassian, spoke modern Greek, it was to him that she came for her too-audible confessions, legendary among the seminarians. Maria always took up her position for prayer directly in front of the prominent Calvary for the dead, repeatedly kissing the image of Christ, of the most holy Godbirthgiver and of St. John, and never, it seemed to me, even for a single minute, ceasing to cross herself.

I even recall hearing the muffled arguments accompanying one of her legendary confessions. It was the night of Holy Pascha, while the *Canon of the Harrowing of Hell* was being sung at the beginning of the long service. Above the solemn Russian chanting, raised voices were heard engaged in a spirited dialogue between the bishop and little Old-Calendarist Maria. In getting shriven, she was anything but passive with her distinguished confessor, objecting, correcting, and striving to be sure he understood exactly what she was trying to convey.

Then, even more luminous than ever, she emerged after her confession, a tiny smiling figure, radiant with light. Throughout the whole long liturgy, she seemed to continue to radiate the holy light of Pascha, even as she did afterwards as we moved downstairs to the Pascal table set up in the seminary refectory where I, too, had been invited as a guest that evening. Never ceasing to beam with joy at any who looked at her, she also seemed, on the slightest provocation, to cross herself yet again in gratitude just for existing and just for being there at the Lord's Pascal feast. When the meal had ended and the Bishop, clergy, seminarians and guests started retiring from the table, I caught sight of little black-clad, Old-Calendarist, "right glory" Maria making her way up the steps to the temple above, a rolled-up pallet under her arm. There, before the Lord in His temple and, I suspect, right in front of the Calvary where she was wont to pray, little Old-Calendarist Maria, full of the right glory of the Resurrection, would sleep, awaiting the dawn of Easter morning.

I have also seen in London, Ontario, a "right glory" elderly Greek lady of distinction and great dignity, not at all given to making a display of herself, on Holy Thursday evening after the church had cleared and all others had venerated the image of the Crucified set up in front, quietly go to the back of the church and kneel down at the beginning of the long aisle leading up to the image. Creeping on her knees, she slowly, painfully made her way up to the image to prostrate herself and venerate the Crucified with tears and kisses. Indeed, I learned also that this same remarkable lady, who came from a nearby town, found herself alone on the morning of February 2 at our local Greek parish for the Feast of the Meeting of the Lord in the Temple. Our city, unlike her own town, had been struck overnight with an extremely severe snowstorm that had stopped local buses. Undaunted, her intrepid young son had somehow managed to deposit his mother at the church, where she found only the professional chanter. He preemptively announced to her that there would be no church that day, for the priest had just called to say he could not get out of his driveway and so he, the chanter, was now going home. The "right glory" lady quietly replied that she was going to stay. She asked the chanter, before he left, to set the church door to lock itself after her departure and to mark the books on the chanter's stand for the texts necessary for singing Matins of the feast. As the door closed behind the departing chanter that morning in the local Greek parish, the "right glory" elderly Greek lady, in all her reserve and dignity, quietly mounted the chanter's stand and, arming herself with the sign of the cross, proceeded to sing Matins, priest or no priest, giving "right glory" to the Lord's Presentation in the Temple, accompanied not by men but by angels.

Finally, I might also recall in that same Greek-Canadian parish a very pious and slightly eccentric young Greek woman. She was, like the Old Calendarist in Paris, also named Maria, and she left on me an equally indelible and unique impression of "right glory." She was humbly employed as a sorely underpaid dishwasher at a Catholic boarding school. When the priest failed to turn up for one of the five Fridays in Lent for singing the *Akathist*, Maria declined to join the other women in sitting down and quietly chatting before going home. Procuring a lighted candle, which she clutched in one hand, and with her *Akathist* text in the other, she placed herself in front of the icon of the most holy Godbirthgiver that had been set out for the service. All on her own, she started singing the praises, one after the other:

Hail thou through whom joy shall shine forth!
Hail thou through whom the curse shall be blotted out!
Hail thou, the restoration of the fallen Adam!
Hail thou, the redemption of the tears of Eve!

Hail thou bride unwedded!

This exercise in single-minded devotion did not seem to stir much response among the pious women present, since Maria always seemed to put them off by being such a unique being. It must be admitted, of course, that the sounds Maria produced would have discouraged even the most musical of them from trying to join her in chanting the praises, for she truly seemed to have no sense of tone whatsoever, Byzantine, Western or otherwise. Yet there she stood, showing forth the "right glory" of Holy Orthodoxy as she discordantly -- at times even gratingly -- sang as best she could the lines of that highly spiritual text that a modern Greek poet has termed "the jewel of Byzantine poetry," even though it was being sung in a Byzantine tone to which God alone could have assigned a name.

A few weeks later, I saw Maria for the last time. She had placed herself at the church doors following the Pascal Liturgy and was busily distributing cheap little paper icons of the Resurrection to every member of the congregation as they emerged. Shortly thereafter, she disappeared from our city, probably to return to Greece. Be that as it may, I have now, for almost 40 years, piously preserved in my Holy Week book that poor, cheap little paper image handed to me that night of Holy Pascha. Remembering her "right glory" witness before God, I cross myself and kiss it, then turn it over to read once more the English greeting she had scrawled in her uneducated handwriting on the back: "Christ is risen, my friend, He really has risen!"

These humble, homely images of "right glory" were not born out of any intellectual activity of "right belief" or "right doctrine," but sprang from an interior source rooted in the heart of the believer. Though it goes without saying that they all these pious women profoundly believed the "right teaching" and "right doctrine" of the Holy Orthodox faith, I discovered in them, as I sought Christ, something quite inexplicable and going far beyond either "right teaching" or "right doctrine." For the Holy Spirit, "*the Lord and Giver of life*," prompted them to go forward and stretch life a bit beyond its usual limits and hesitations and, in their own way, a way coming purely from their heart, to proclaim, before men and angels, the glory that He Himself had made manifest in their hearts.

Because all these believers loved Christ, that glory welled up in them on these occasions, spilling out and overflowing into creation around them so that I, an unworthy sinner seeking Christ, might behold, burning in their hearts, all the glory and all the fair beauty of the Lord. They had truly become "living epistles," since the word of Christ had been indelibly graven in their hearts not with ink but, as the holy Apostle states, by the burning Spirit of the living God.

CHAPTER IV

The Heart of Being Countercultural

The clash between Orthodox Christianity and the culture of the world has always been dramatic. It often has been far more spectacular than it is presently in North American culture, where anti-Christian feeling, though quite effective in its snide denigration and insinuations in the media, does not yet involve systematic imprisonment, torture, execution and confiscation of the property of arrested Christians.

Such rules did prevail, however, throughout the first three centuries of Christian history as merciless, sporadic persecutions revealed the desire of the Roman Empire to eradicate the pernicious new religion centered on the resurrected Galilean. Paradoxically, however, it was also during those first three centuries that the new, counterculture religion spread at an astounding rate throughout the confines of the vast Roman Empire.

Certainly nothing could have been further removed from the official pantheistic state religion, with its deification of Emperors and mandatory state-imposed cult for worshipping them, than was the Gospel of Jesus Christ. The Roman world believed that claims made about the Incarnation of God in Jesus Christ were totally false, just as non-believers still hold to this day. The official Roman government had, after all, at the request of the Jewish establishment in Jerusalem, put Jesus Christ to death as a criminal. As for the preposterous rumor of His having risen from the dead on the third day, the Roman world reasoned that it could only be precisely just that: a preposterous rumor. Was it not completely contrary to the natural and universal order of things?

Whereas the Roman Empire during those first three centuries confidently felt authorized to create new gods by deifying its emperors, Christians paradoxically discovered in Jesus Christ's shameful criminal's death a life-giving strength. Again and again before their torturers they demonstrated their belief that it was His ever-present, risen life dwelling in them that sustained them.

This is graphically illustrated in the eyewitness account of the North African martyrdom of St. Felicity, taking place in Carthage around 203, during the reign of Valerian. A bondservant and Christian catechumen, Felicity died for Christ in the arena along with her catechist, Saturis, and four fellow-catechumens, only one of which was female. This was the 22-year-old noble lady, Perpetua, who had brought her nursing infant with her into prison. When all six were condemned to the beasts, Felicity, eight months pregnant, was distressed at the possibility of her own martyrdom being postponed until after the birth of her child, separating her witness from that of her catechist and four fellow-catechumens.

Three days before their scheduled confrontation with the wild beasts, however, and as if in answer to her own and her companions' fervent prayers that they not be separated in their witness, Felicity went into labor. An insensitive jailer, overhearing her groans, cruelly mocked her, promising her far worse pains shortly to come. Felicity, with great conviction and presence of mind, replied: "*Now it is I who suffer what I am suffering, but in that hour Another will be suffering in me, for what I shall be suffering then shall be for Him!*"

On the scheduled day, Perpetua and Felicity, having confided their babes to a Christian woman who visited them in prison, were the last two of the six martyrs to perish. Each of the four men had already been slain by a different beast when an enraged cow was released on the two young women. The frantic, crazed bovine tossed Perpetua into the air but, failing to kill either of them, was removed from the arena. The spectators then saw the noble Perpetua approach the bondservant, Felicity, to exchange with her the Christian kiss of peace just as a sword-bearing gladiator-executioner appeared. As though she were a lamb for sacrifice, he quickly dispatched Felicity the bondservant by slitting her throat. Before the noble Perpetua, however, he flinched. She, with calm and determined presence of mind, firmly seized his hand, then deliberately guided the blade to her throat.

ii

As this moving eyewitness account reveals, the Roman Empire was pitted against a seemingly irresistible force of counterculture released into the world by the coming of Jesus of Nazareth who, the martyrs were convinced, was actually suffering in them. This consistent comportment on the part of the disciples of the Nazarene defied all logic and human reasoning.

Where had mighty Rome failed? From the beginning, she had done her official best to suppress Him. In accordance with the riotous outcries of the Jews of Jerusalem before the Roman governor, Pontius Pilate, that He be crucified, He had indeed been nailed to a Roman cross and pierced to the heart by the spear of the Roman centurion that Pilate had charged with heading the execution squad. Once Pilate had been reassured of the Nazarene's death, this same centurion was further entrusted by the Roman governor with having his soldiers guard the grave of the crucified "King of the Jews," who had foretold that He would rise on the third day. The Jews of Jerusalem feared, therefore, that Jesus' disciples might come and steal His body away so that they might then claim that He had indeed risen from the dead.

The details given in the Gospels about Jesus' legs not being broken not only are a fulfillment of Jewish prophecy, but also lend considerable weight to the veracity of the Centurion's testimony that Jesus had indeed died on the cross. For those who died by crucifixion, it was not slowly bleeding to death that was the cause of death, but suffocation. Being suspended with one's arms stretched above the head inevitably causes the lungs to fill with fluid. Only by the victim's pushing on his legs, thereby raising his body upwards and bringing his head to the level of his arms and allowing the lungs to be cleared, can temporary relief can be achieved.[3] It

---

[3] Two distinctly different blood-flows, obviously due to these two quite normal positions taken by a crucified victim, are still visible on the arm-prints of the holy Shroud of Turin. One flows the full length of the upstretched arm, while the other shows that the victim, having raised himself, caused the blood to flow straight down from the pierced wrists, rather than running down the arms. This is but one of numerous details pointing to the authenticity of this holy relic, the primary one being the position of the nail-prints in the wrists and not in the palms, something unheard

becomes obvious then that once the victim, because of broken legs, could no longer raise himself to clear his lungs, they would rapidly fill and suffocation would follow. The order to break the legs of the crucified was, everyone knew, tantamount to an order for immediate death.

The Jews, not wanting the agony of the three crucified victims to pollute the Sabbath that was beginning at sunset, asked Pilate to have their legs broken. At this point, the experienced Roman execution squad ascertained that Jesus had already died and, therefore, broke only the legs of the two thieves crucified with Him. The Centurion in charge, however, conscious of his responsibility towards the Roman governor, nonetheless made a point of giving a deadly thrust with his spear to the heart of the Nazarene and himself immediately witnessed blood and water flow out, thereby fulfilling yet another Jewish prophecy (Zac 12:10). Thus might he affirm, as the most reliable witness possible and the one responsible for the execution, that the Roman sentence of death had been fully carried out: Jesus of Nazareth had really and truly died on the cross.

iii

Once He was dead, the Jews' anguished, obsessive concern became fixated on their fear that His disciples would steal away His body from the grave and claim that He had risen from the dead. Struggling doggedly to maintain the authority of the Jewish temple, which, through the power of the Spirit of God and within the divine economy, was already actually being superseded by the new era of Jesus Christ, the Jews in Jerusalem were not about to yield their considerable authority if it could possibly be protected, even if they had grasped Jesus' reference to the Resurrection when He said to them: "*Destroy this temple and in three days I will raise it up*" (Jn 2:19). They petitioned Pilate to have the Centurion and his men maintain an all-night vigil over the grave of Jesus Christ. This squad,

---

of at the time that the so-called "forgery" was supposedly made. For a recent explanation of why the carbon-dating test of the Holy Shroud should not be considered conclusive, see: Dr. Leoncio A. Garza-Valdes. *The DNA of God?* (1999, Doubleday: New York) ISBN: 0-385-48850-5.

representing the great might of the all-powerful Roman Empire put at the service of the Jewish temple establishment in Jerusalem, was able not only to guarantee that Jesus Christ had truly died on the cross, but also to certify that his disciples had definitely not sneaked into the tomb that night to steal His body away.

This official Roman contingent, charged with the execution and all-night vigil over the grave, were the unwitting witnesses to any number of strange and unusual happenings surrounding the Galilean's death and burial. Moreover, the Centurion and two of his men seem to have grasped that these strange events were somehow related to His death and to Who He was. Whether the darkening of the sun at mid-day during the crucifixion, the earthquake and opening of tombs with the dead coming forth and appearing in the city, or the great burst of glory issuing forth from the tomb and leaving it empty and the shroud still intact within, these things, they knew, had taken place. Quite rightly, the officials of the temple grasped that if it could be claimed that He had risen from the dead, their current state of affairs could become far worse than they had been concerning the crucified Jesus of Nazareth.

The tradition recounting the fate of that Centurion and two of his men who, like him, believed that they had actually participated in the crucifixion of the "Son of God," adds depth to our own understanding of the frightening challenge posed to imperial Roman culture and its civil religion by the divine revelation of God in Jesus Christ. It is of significance that "*the centurion which stood over against him [...]*" and said, "*Truly this was the Son of God*" (Mk 15:39), did indeed go on to become a martyr himself for this truth. As an eyewitness to the death and resurrection, he was actually far better situated to know exactly what had happened than any of the Apostles. It is particularly moving for us today to think that he was not a Jew, but a pagan Roman who had no idea whatsoever of the existence of those Jewish prophecies he and his men helped fulfill in such remarkable detail.

His name was Longinus. The large bribes offered the Roman soldiers by the Jews to say that the body of Jesus had been stolen were flatly rejected both by Longinus and by the two men of his squad who shared his conviction that the crucified Jesus of Nazareth was truly the Son of God. They immediately left Roman service and made their way back to Longinus's native Cappadocia.

The defection of Longinus with two of his soldiers was immediately reported by Pontius Pilate to the emperor, Tiberius, in Rome. With orders to destroy Longinus, soldiers were dispatched to Cappadocia where, according to tradition, Longinus actually found himself playing host to his unsuspecting executioners in his own home. He received them hospitably and, upon learning their mission, excused himself to go make preparations for his burial, as well as to alert his two brother soldiers. Both opted to share in his martyrdom. All having been made ready, Longinus announced his identity to his appreciative guests, who were reluctant to slaughter so gracious a host. He urged them, as true Romans, to do their duty with no further delay. His head was dispatched to Pilate in Jerusalem.

iv

We know, of course, that the unbelievable and utterly inexplicable power of the Holy Spirit, ever emanating from the risen Christ, had brought the mighty world empire of Rome to its knees before Him three centuries later. Even the Emperor himself, Constantine the Great, worshipped the risen Christ as God. The Resurrection was no longer regarded as a "preposterous rumor, " but an established historical fact, the proofs of which, to this day, it is interesting to note, are rehearsed in song and text, Sunday after Sunday throughout the world, wherever Matins are sung in an Orthodox Church.

Not only had Jesus Christ repeatedly foretold that He would rise from the dead on the third day, but after this event, He repeatedly manifested Himself to His disciples and apostles over a period of 40 days. He was, in fact, seen by many before taking public leave of his followers on the 40th day on the Mount of Olives. There, He was taken from their sight after having promised to be with them until the end of the world.

As Longinus and his two companions had witnessed, some new and unusual power had been released in the world by the coming of this new god, Jesus of Nazareth. Fifty days after His Resurrection and just ten days after being taken up into heaven, His disciples and apostles, along

50

with His mother, were, according to His instructions, all assembled together in continuing prayer in Jerusalem on the Jewish feast of Pentecost, when they experienced a strange and powerful outpouring of the Holy Spirit. The ability to make oneself understood in a language other than one's own was mysteriously experienced by His followers, who at once began to proclaim Jesus Christ as the risen Son of God to the thousands of fervent Jews and Jewish converts who had assembled in Jerusalem for the feast.

As a result of this preaching, thousands were baptized. The mass enthusiasm of the many converts made that day, as well as the witness given shortly thereafter by the glorious martyrdom of St. Stephen, followed by the miraculous conversion of that ferocious persecutor of Christians, Saul of Tarsus, all seemed to confirm the "preposterous rumor" of the Resurrection of the Nazarene. Moreover, the unrelenting spread of this quite extraordinary story of a miraculous Resurrection throughout the whole of the Roman Empire by those Pentecost-converts as they returned home to their countries. from Jerusalem was in no way lessened by the Pentecost-inflamed disciples, who themselves also fanned out from Jerusalem, proclaiming the good news of victory over death through Jesus Christ. Like a wind-whipped forest fire, the unbelievable story of death having been conquered by Jesus had proven uncontainable.

It was natural, of course, that the new religion involving the risen crucified God from Nazareth was initially identified primarily with the Jewish diaspora among which it was taking root. Followers of the Galilean were regarded as members of a new Jewish sect and widely suppressed, first by the Jewish establishment in Jerusalem, then by the Roman government. As is well known, the Emperor Nero blamed Christians for the burning of Rome.

One dares not dwell upon the hideousness of the desperate, writhing agony inflicted on all those Christians Nero ordered to be attached to poles, covered in pitch, and set aflame as human torches to illumine his evening revelries. The degenerate and brutal pagan society that Christianity was destined to replace obviously did not recoil from the horrors of utilizing human torches to illuminate its passionately pursued pleasures.

THE HEART OF ORTHODOX MYSTERY

The severity with which not only Nero, but numerous subsequent Roman Emperors sporadically persecuted the new Jewish sect, right up to the beginning of the fourth century and the coming of Constantine, can only betray imperial Rome's prescient and, as it were, instinctive uneasiness before what seemed to have burst into the world since the obscure, crucified Nazarene from Galilee had supposedly risen from the dead. The ferocity and cruelty of the tortures routinely applied under Roman law, not just to Christian men, but also to women and even to children, reflect the fear the mighty Roman government felt from the beliefs of the followers of this new Jewish god whom believers called "the Christ," that is "the Anointed One." Did they somehow sense that their whole culture, indeed the entire familiar pagan culture of all the vast ancient world, was now about to crumble as had never happened before in the history of mankind? Before even the humblest disciples of the Crucified One the mighty Roman Empire shrank back in measured contempt.

Particularly noxious to Roman culture was Christianity's emphasis on consecrated virginity, something viewed as harmful to the well-being of the Empire. The highly honored Vestal Virgins were one thing, but their number was strictly limited, and once their career was finished, they could marry if they wished. But having dozens of young women of rank and education actually insisting on a whole life devoted to celibacy and physical austerity, often shared with women of lower estate, could only be viewed by the Roman government as anti-patriotic, seditious, and subversive. Certainly it was countercultural. Were they not thereby refusing to produce children for the expansion of the Roman Empire in consecrating their virginity to the One they called the "heavenly Bridegroom," Jesus Christ?

The most frequent cause for torture and martyrdom, however, turned out to be the quiet, firm refusal of Christians of all ages, gender, or social condition to offer a token pinch of incense before representations of the pagan gods, among which often figured the portrait of the latest deified Emperor. For refusing to honor the gods of the Roman pantheon, and thereby rejecting the very basis of Roman culture, the Christians were, in their counterculture, termed "atheists." As far as Rome was concerned, her pantheon was always open to placing the representation of the Nazarene alongside all the other gods, only there seemed to be no pleasing these disgruntled, trouble-making Christians. They flatly refused, again confirming that they were indeed profoundly, irretrievably, and definitively countercultural.

V

Time and again, martyred Christians vainly pointed out that the God they served was not just another god of the Roman Pantheon, but the One True God, the Almighty, the Creator of all things. Was it reasonable to ask them, who served such a Creator-God, to pay honor to graven images or gold-plated statues fashioned by human creatures like themselves? True to their monotheistic Jewish roots, Christians stubbornly allowed for only one, lone divinity. That the Romans consequently regarded Christians as "atheists" for refusing to recognize the familiar, time-honored gods of Rome is graphically illustrated for us by the second century eyewitness account we have of the martyrdom of the venerable Bishop of Smyrna, St. Polycarp.

This charismatic 86-year-old bishop of Smyrna was the last known disciple of St. John the Theologian, who himself had been the last surviving Apostle, dying at Ephesus only at the end of the first century. Polycarp, with his older brother-disciple, Boucolos, had actually shared the first part of the beloved John's ministry, prior to John's being arrested and exiled to Patmos. The old Apostle had, however, ordained Boucolos as the first Bishop of Smyrna and dispatched the younger Polycarp with him as a priest to that new see in Asia Minor.

Many years later, during a rash of persecution at Smyrna, Polycarp, now in his eighties and himself a much venerated bishop, was arrested on Good Friday after having had a dream that caused him to remark to his disciples that he now understood that he would die by fire. At his entrance into the arena of the amphitheatre, the Christians present reported hearing a voice say, "*Be brave, Polycarp, and act as a man!*" as the old bishop painfully made his way to the center to stand before the imperial box.

From there, the Roman proconsul, visibly moved by the old man's frailty, interrogated the venerable figure standing below him down in the

53

arena. Aware of what the old man what was about to undergo for his faith, the proconsul tried to reason with him to spare himself.

"*Take pity on your many years!*" he said. "*Swear by the fortune of Caesar and say, 'Down with the atheists!'*"

Slowly, the old man raised his eyes to the highest rows of the amphitheatre, taking in the crowd of pagans surrounding him and filling every seat. He answered the proconsul with a sigh, "*Yes indeed! Down with the atheists!*"

But when the proconsul asked him to curse Christ, Polycarp quietly refused, saying, "*For 86 years I have served Him, and He has never done me any harm. How can I possibly blaspheme my King and my Saviour?*"

Frustrated in his impotence to sway the old man, the proconsul threatened him, "*I have wild beasts,*" he called down menacingly to Polycarp. "*Change your mind or I shall feed you to them.*"

Confidently and without flinching, Polycarp calmly answered, "*Bring them on. It is impossible for us to change our minds and go from something better to something worse. But it is good to change if we pass from evil to righteousness.*"

Trying to regain the dominant position, the proconsul said testily, "*Since you scorn the wild beasts, I shall burn you with fire if you don't change your mind.*"

Upon hearing the word "fire," Polycarp was suddenly filled with joy, for he remembered his dream. He smiled as he answered, "*You threaten me with a fire that burns for a moment, but is extinguished shortly thereafter. You know nothing of the fire of the judgment to come, nor of the eternal torment awaiting the impious. So why wait longer? Go ahead and do what you will.*"

Then, when the herald had proclaimed three times that Polycarp had declared himself a Christian, the infuriated crowd demanded that a lion be set loose upon him. But upon being advised that the animal games for that day had already come to an end, the crowd spontaneously began shouting, "*Let Polycarp be burnt alive! Let Polycarp be burnt alive!*"

This cry came from every side of the arena. In an instant, the pagans and Jews, in complete disorder, started getting to their feet to go search for wood and fagots for the pyre. As soon as wood from nearby workshops and baths had been amassed in the amphitheatre to form the pyre, Polycarp himself, as if he were preparing to celebrate the Holy Sacrifice, calmly laid aside his outer garments. He even insisted on removing his shoes, something he never normally did, since the faithful were always pressing around him to kiss his feet. However, when they wanted to nail him to the stake, he refused.

"*Leave me as I am,*" he said. "*He who gives me the strength to stand the fire will give me strength also to remain on the pyre without moving.*"

Placed on the wood like a choice victim prepared for holocaust, Polycarp raised his eyes to heaven and thanked God in a last prayer for having judged him worthy, in the incorruptibility of the Holy Spirit, now, along with all the holy martyrs, to partake of the chalice of Christ for Resurrection and Eternal Life.

As soon as he had pronounced "*Amen,*" the executioners lighted the pyre and a great flame rose up. But, as if by a miracle, the fire took on the appearance of a vault, completely surrounding the body of the martyr like a rampart, or a ship's sail swollen by the wind. In the midst of it stood Polycarp, like bread being baked, or like gold or silver being purified in the furnace, not at all giving off the stench of burning flesh, but rather the sweet odor of incense or precious aromatics. The impious, seeing that the saint's body was not being consumed, ordered the executioner to finish him off with a spear. Blood gushed out in such quantity that the fire was completely extinguished, leaving the crowd stupefied.

At the insistence of the Jews, the precious remains of the martyr were burned, though the faithful did manage to save some bones, which they placed in an appropriate place. There, every year, they joyously gathered to celebrate the anniversary of Polycarp's heavenly birth. For a few months, the glorious martyrdom of the venerable Polycarp caused the anti-Christian persecution to cease.

vi

The challenge to worldly culture so graphically expressed in the eyewitness account of the martyrdom of St. Polycarp might seem far more extreme to today's reader than any challenge presently faced in North

America. The fact is, however, that the mystery of Christ and His Church is always a challenge to worldly culture in any age and in any country. The reaction of the world may vary, of course, but the inevitable basic challenge of Orthodox Christianity always representing a counterculture is always there for the lover of Christ.

In fact, the civil religion espoused by the founders of the American Republic and based on the "*inalienable right to life, liberty, and the pursuit of happiness,*" would, no less than the state religion of Rome, be diametrically opposed to a witness such as that of the "glorious martyrdom" of St. Polycarp of Smyrna. Throughout North America, and with no apology whatsoever, does not one, Christian or not, still speak unabashedly of "pursuing happiness?"

Is the "pursuit of happiness" not, according to the myth created by the founding fathers of the American Republic, an "inalienable right?" That concept has, in fact, entered so deeply into the thought and conscience of generations of North Americans that it is difficult to question it without being suspected of being, if not actually some kind of foreign agent, at least "un-American." The concept of "the pursuit of happiness" itself is, however, diametrically opposed to Orthodox Christianity's view of the Christian's fundamentally sacrificial and intercessory role in the cosmos, to say nothing of Christianity's most basic tenant: the sacrifice of Christ is absolutely essential within the divine economy of His Incarnation.

"The pursuit of happiness" actually opposes, moreover, man's intimate relationship with God and that total submission to God the holy fathers of Orthodoxy teach us is basic to the spiritual life. The true lover of Christ, in fact, can never take the concept of the "pursuit of happiness" seriously as something that might ever be incorporated into his own life in Christ.

The "pursuit of happiness" inevitably fosters a totally self-centered view of life, ignoring completely all cosmic sense of man's place in the universe. It further ignores the inevitable, perennial and very basic dimension of sacrifice demanded of man at every level of his human existence. Whether in pursuing the bonds of love with a future spouse, or in bringing forth and rearing children, or in caring for those one loves, or in maintaining the well-being of one's own family, sacrifice and suffering are far more basic necessities to human well-being than is the "pursuit of happiness."

Whence then came this superficiality and shallowness postulating what a government should stand for in regard to its citizens? To a great extent, this shallowness can most certainly be attributed to the 18th century so-called "Enlightenment" of which, intellectually, the Fathers of the American Republic were the too-confident sons.

A direct descendent of Renaissance humanism, the 18th century Enlightenment had strong convictions about what was important and what was not. Man alone, not God, was to be taken seriously and served. Though God was somewhere up above, He was no longer one to reveal Himself to anyone as He did in those far-removed, superstitious, and ancient times of the Bible.

This point of view today still remains basic to the assumptions of officially legislated American culture, the various Christian coalitions so often spoken of in the press notwithstanding. When a conflict arises, such as the question of prayer in schools in America, it is the man-centered preoccupation with North America's Enlightenment heritage that lies behind not only the exclusion of prayers, but even of the mention of God in public schools, as shocking as this would undoubtedly have proven to the deist fathers of the American Republic.

Be that as it may, these founding fathers still, being what they were, kept God at a very respectable distance in the official documents when the American Republic was being set up. This distant God might be invoked, but only to the extent to which He could be used for the benefit of man. Never did He exist for His own sake alone. He could be freely associated with "life," "liberty" and "the pursuit of happiness," since these were, after all, the personal aspirations of all sons of the Enlightenment.[4]

---

[4] One should perhaps note that, in the mid-nineteenth century, Abraham Lincoln bears witness not only to a very personal sense of the omnipotence of God, but also to the eternal justice and righteousness of God as shown in his Second Inaugural Address. There he views the blood of the soldiers being shed in the Civil War as answering the blood shed by the slave-master's lash. Had the prosperity of the new Republic not been, in part at least, guaranteed by slave labor? If, Lincoln reasons, the soldiers' blood was now to pay for the blood of the slaves, then we can only humbly pray before God, "Just art thou in all thy works, O God!"

Even in choosing to believe in God, the Fathers of the Republic still considered themselves the masters of this world and the center of their own self-appointed goal, something that has remained a very "American" characteristic. Certainly, deist man was very far from viewing himself as existing for God, and for God alone, and therefore utterly dependent upon God's grace even to exist. According to the deists, God had made man that man might enjoy the "pursuit of happiness." No lowly sheep of God's pasture, he! Whereas the true lover of Christ, of necessity, views man as fashioned by God, and existing for God alone and not for himself, Enlightenment man refused, and still refuses, such a Christian idea.

Having thus divorced himself from God incarnate in Jesus Christ, deist man was most certainly not about to entertain the possibility that God actually continues, in our modern age, to reveal Himself through Jesus Christ to the saints within the mystery of the Orthodox Church! That the God of the Bible, through divine revelation, actually reveals Himself to man was also completely foreign even to the deist clergy of 18th century France and England, who themselves laid the foundation for completely divorcing educated Westerners from the God of the Bible. Moreover, grave suspicion about revelations even being possible still holds, for the most part, in Western Christianity and can be found at the root of the "modernizing" adherents of Roman Catholicism who insist on official intellectual and scientific analyses, even of the miracles of the saints sent by God Himself.

For such self-centered and proud children of Renaissance humanism, it has become a natural reaction to maintain utter distrust and suspicion, if not downright disbelief, in anything coming from outside oneself. It is not without relevance that leaders of the French Revolution, such as Danton and Robespierre, had all been educated by deist clergy. Those misbegotten cleric-professors, being themselves imbued with the "new ideas," successfully in turn imbued their pupils with far greater admiration for the heroes of ancient Rome than for the Roman martyrs and saints of the Christian Church.

Both Robespierre and Danton merely applied the ideas taught them by their deist cleric-professors. Could there be anything farther removed from the flesh-and-blood Incarnation of Jesus Christ and His mercy to sinners, so sublimely demonstrated in the story of the woman caught in the act of adultery, than that frigid, intellectual "virtue" Robespierre so passionately sought to impose? He was, after all, willing to guillotine anyone he conceived of as getting in the way of realizing his impossible dream of establishing a truly virtuous French republic. During the last six weeks of the Great Terror, Robespierre's crusade for "virtue" sent 1,306 persons to the guillotine in Paris alone, among whom are found few aristocrats or clergy.

Paradoxically, the fruit borne by those 18th century deist cleric-professors is, moreover, not only to be found in the French Revolution, but also in its nefarious dissemination throughout the world, particularly in the rise of Communism. Many of those upheavals, by the vastness of the catastrophes resulting from them, cause the French Revolution to seem but a sort of tranquil prelude to an overwhelming, subsequent tragedy. Paris's brief, four-month Reign of Terror under Robespierre is hardly worth mentioning when compared with the Ukrainian famine created by the Soviet Union, for example, or, more recently, the genocide produced by the Khmer Rouge in Cambodia.

In any case, living for Jesus Christ alone was, indeed, something fundamentally opposed to the thinking of the framers of the American Constitution, whatever their merits as lawgivers. Having rejected Christ and His saints, any idea of seeking to live within the mystery of Christ's Church would necessarily have been regarded as something completely useless and irrelevant, as it still is by non-believers to this day. It is this rejection of Christ by the world that continues to make Orthodoxy radically countercultural, just as it always has, in fact, since the Prince of this world is not Christ.

The challenge offered immigrant Orthodox Christians in regard to civil religion in America has always come, and still comes, from their desire not only to survive, but to "fit in" to North American cultural patterns and somehow not prove to be countercultural. How many well-meaning immigrant Orthodox, wishing sincerely to pay grateful and quite genuine homage to the freedom they have received as American citizens, struggle gallantly to accommodate the American Republic's officially enshrined ideal of the "pursuit of happiness" as a realistic goal for living out their life in the new country? Having experienced so many good things that were often denied them or completely impossible ever to achieve in an older and ethnically Orthodox country that, perhaps, had fallen under Communist control, they find themselves torn between the unswerving Orthodoxy of their grandmothers and the American idealism of the "pursuit of happiness" espoused by their energetic and successful Americanized offspring, of whom they are so justly proud.

The great national feast of Thanksgiving Day, always arriving with its "turkey and all the trimmings" in the midst of Christmas Lent, is perhaps the most notable conflict imposed on Orthodox Christians by American's civil religion. I was told by a friend about a visit to some old Greek-American friends during Great Lent. He noticed that the parents were keeping the fast, but that their teenage children were eating meat. When asked why this was so, the parents answered him with confidence and great pride: "Americans do not fast, and our children are Americans!"

For the convert-lover of Christ who opts for Orthodoxy, a fairly basic and all-inclusive question, therefore, must inevitably arise, sooner or later: "Is the Incarnation of God in Jesus Christ worth sacrificing one's whole life for?"

Embodied in this question is the implacable challenge offered, at all times and in all places, to every believer by the ongoing mystery of the Church. This challenge takes us far beyond all the superficial details of Orthodox lifestyle and far beyond the American dream of the pursuit of happiness. This question, in fact, uncompromisingly articulates the ongoing countercultural challenge required of anyone who, through Christ, seeks to understand the value not only of his own human life, but also the value of the life of all those around him.

The historical fact that God was made man in Jesus Christ, therefore, becomes, in light of this question, "*the still point of the turning world*," as T. S. Eliot put it. The Incarnation, that "*still point of the turning world*," contains within itself the Logos and only-begotten Son and Word of God, the beginning and end of creation itself. The veritable challenge that must be faced squarely, day-by-day in Christian living is that of not allowing the demands of civil religion to alter our allegiance to Him Who is our Life and is the only means of saving each of us from the death that is our own nothingness.

CHAPTER V

The Heart of the Uncreated

At the beginning of the fourth century, scarcely a decade before Constantine the Great liberated Christian prisoners from the mines and brought government persecution to an end, the worst attack on the Church yet was launched by the Emperor Diocletian in 303. All property belonging to Christians could be confiscated by the state if they refused to deny Christ by swearing allegiance to the gods of the Roman empire.

This, in fact, had been the fate of the well-off grandparents of St. Basil the Great.

At the time of Diocletian's decree, there lived in Caesarea of Cappadocia, where St. Basil would be named bishop a half-century later, a pious, very wealthy widow named Julitta. She had vast holdings at home and abroad: estates, whole villages, numerous slaves and herds. An unscrupulous but prominent man in Caesarea, coveting her great wealth, had managed by fraudulent means to gain control of all Julitta's holdings. The fraudulent tactics of the culprit were so evident that, when she brought him to justice, Julitta felt sure of regaining control her possessions.

The imperial edict against Christians having just been promulgated, however, the unscrupulous man opportunely denounced Julitta as a Christian before the judge. The judge at once ordered that a portable altar and incense be brought. He then invited Julitta, since she wished the protection of Roman law, to offer incense to the gods of the Roman Empire.

Realizing full well what was now at stake and that the moment of truth had come, Julitta, without hesitating, bowed before the will of God, boldly declaring, "*Let them all be lost then! Riches, glory, or life itself, let all of it disappear! Nothing shall make me deny my Creator and my God who made all things!*" Thereafter, Julitta's only reply to the judge's questions was, "*I am the servant of Christ!*"

Julitta's heroic behavior merited her the judge's irritated condemnation to die by fire. On her way to the pyre, which had been quickly constructed from wood and faggots collected by the crowd here and there, Julitta admonished the women she passed: "*We are created in the same way as men!... Like men we too are created in the image of God!... Strength is as accessible to women as to men!... We too are flesh of Adam's flesh and bone of his bones and we too must offer the Lord a virile constance, a virile courage and virile patience...*"

As if entering into the most luminous bridal chamber, Julitta mounted the pyre. The flames immediately embraced her as her soul sped away quickly to heaven. Her body, however, did not burn and remained intact, as if to indicate the incorruptibility of the elect. On the site of her martyrdom, a basilica was later constructed. Within its atrium, a spring of miracle-working waters welled up. A half century later, St. Basil the Great, as bishop of Caesarea, honored the witness of St. Julitta in a sermon we still possess.

During the long conflict between Rome's civil religion and the early martyrs such as St. Julitta, eyewitnesses report consistently that the martyrs frequently made references to their tormentors that the Roman gods they were supposed to worship had been created by men. They, as Christians, worshipped only the Creator Himself. This argument could not but have perplexed their tormentors. Was the Christian God not the crucified Nazarene, Jesus Christ? How could they possibly claim for Him those attributes given him by Saint Julitta: "*my Creator and my God who made all things?*"

As much as it may surprise us today, early Christians had no hesitation in seeing in Jesus Christ something far beyond a mere crucified Galilean who rose from the dead. They knew Him to be the only-begotten Son and Word of God, the Second Person of the Holy Trinity, made man by the power of the Holy Spirit and the Virgin Mary. In the very first lines of his Gospel's prologue on the Logos, or Word of God, St. John the beloved insists "*all things were made by Him and without Him was not anything made that was made.*" That very basic Christian theology was reiterated again and again not only by St. Paul, but also by all the writers of the New Testament. References to Jesus Christ as "Creator" are, moreover, frequently discovered in the eyewitness accounts of many of the early martyrs.

Those early martyrs were, in fact, even more radically revolutionary in their time than they appear to us today. Like Orthodox Christians today, they clung to a solid theology of the Incarnation of Almighty God in Jesus Christ. Such a truth not only directly challenged the pantheism of Roman state religion, but, even more seriously, they were, for the first time, introducing into the Gentile world the uncreated, almighty and living God of Abraham, Isaac and Jacob. Just as it is today with non-believers, those who were neither Christians nor Jews could conceive of the created order alone, that order submitted to the Prince of this world, where man feels free to fashion his gods after his own likeness and change from one to another according to his own whims and humors. The whole concept of one single and exclusive omnipotent Creator God seemed very foreign to anything the pagan world could imagine.

ii

For those early Christians, as for Orthodox Christians today, man's basic -- one might even say man's "natural" -- tendency towards idolatry was being pitted against concrete, historical facts foreseen by the prophets of Israel and presented to the world in the person of Jesus Christ. He, the Logos of God, by Whom all things were made and "*without [Whom] was not any thing made that was made*" (Jn 1:3), had come to show men the glory He had with the Father from before the creation of the world and, through those who were drawn to love Him and felt called to follow Him, to assure, even to the end of the world, the presence of His uncreated glory in the fallen world. Thus would He, in the power of His glory, and until His return at the end of time, continue to be experienced and manifested in the world by all those who, through their love for Him, are truly His and in whom He dwells.

The very solid Christianity of those early martyrs is, indeed, striking. They had no difficulty in understanding that the Incarnation of God in Jesus Christ had brought man, once and for all, face to face with the Creator, that is, with the Uncreated. It was, thus, His glory as the Uncreated Logos and Word of the Father that shone forth through them as they bore witness to Him and to His glory. It was for the Uncreated only-begotten

Son of God alone that they underwent, again and again, the most frightful and hideous tortures, the account of which still causes us to pale in reading them. Yet, because of the crucified God-Man of the new Christian cult, those early martyrs viewed their torture and death at the hands of their Roman tormentors as the most glorious crowning possible of their earthly life.

On this point, the very moving martyrdom of the 40 martyrs of Sebastia is particularly instructive. It was actually the great devotion of St. Basil the Great's own mother to the 40 Martyrs that caused the first church dedicated to them to be erected.

This notable martyrdom came about when Agricolaos was sent as the resident magistrate to Sebastia to enforce the decree saying that Christians must either conform to the law or be submitted to terrible tortures. With Agricolaos came the 12th Roman Legion to provide the military might needed to enforce the cruel, universal decree.

Forty soldiers of that 12th Legion, however, were themselves secretly Christians, not one of which was not young and brave and much appreciated for his services. When it was demanded that they sacrifice to the gods of the Empire, they all refused, each one in turn declaring before Agricolas, "*I am a Christian.*"

Hoping to win them over through kindness, Agricolaos praised them for their valor, promising them, if they would submit, advantages and favors from the Emperor himself. Though the 40 young Christians were of very different origins and from various parts of the Empire, they proved one in faith, showing great solidarity with the spokesman who spoke on their behalf to Agricolaos:

"*If, as you say, we have fought valiantly for the Emperor of the world, how much more valiantly must we now fight out of love for Him who is the Ruler of the whole universe! There is only one life for us now: death for Christ.*"

Thrown into prison, the 40 young Christian legionnaires fell on their knees, praying to the Lord to keep them in the true faith and to strengthen them in their coming struggle. As they continued to sing psalms throughout the night, the Lord appeared to them, saying, "*You have begun well, but only to him who perseveres to the end will the crown be granted!*"

The next morning, they were again brought before Agricolaos. His renewed flatteries were interrupted by one of their number, Candidus, who openly accused him of hypocritical sweetness. Agricolaos was greatly irritated but could not yet pronounce his sentence in the absence of the Legion's general, Lysias. As the accused awaited the decisive confrontation with their general, one of the legionnaires, named Quirion, encouraged the others, saying, *"We have three enemies, the devil, Lysios and Agricolaos. Nonetheless, what can they do against us as forty soldiers of Jesus Christ?"*

Upon his return, Lysias's immediate reaction to the firmness and resolve of his 40 recalcitrant men was to order the other legionnaires to take up stones and smash the teeth of the 40 Christians. Immediately, the stone-bearing legionnaires threw themselves on the Christians. Blinded by divine power, however, they found themselves striking each other. Lysias, enraged at this ridiculous twist of circumstances, himself hurled a stone at the saints only to have it strike Agricolaos, seriously wounding him. The 40 Christians were herded back to their prison while the governor pondered an appropriate form of execution for them.

Plunging the depths of his perverse imagination, Agricolaos the next day ordered that the 40 Christians all be taken just outside Sebastia to a frozen lake, stripped naked, and forced to spend the night out on the ice. The saints, upon arriving at the frozen lake, rivaled one another in stripping off their clothes, saying, *"What can we render to the Lord for what He suffered for our salvation? Soldiers stripped Him naked, so let us now strip ourselves of our garments that the military order be pardoned!"* They further reasoned, *"Come what may, this corruptible body must die, so let us now accept to die of our own free will that we may live eternally! Receive, O Lord, this holocaust that will be consumed by cold rather than by fire!"*

As a single man, the 40 Christians went out onto the ice. Throughout the night, as they endured the bite of the glacial wind, they kept praying that just as they numbered 40 in entering into this contest, so might they also emerge from it still numbering 40.

Agricolaos also had had the fiendish inspiration to set up a steaming bath cabin on the lakeshore to tempt the Christians. Indeed, one of the 40 succumbed to the temptation and rushed off the ice to enter it, only to meet his death from the too-sudden change in temperature. As the

39 left on the lake redoubled their prayers to hold fast in their struggle, a sudden light pierced the night sky, hovering over them and warming them. Angels became visible, descending to place resplendent crowns on the 39 heads.

It was at this point that one of the guards, warming himself by the bath cabin, spotted a 40th crown suspended in the air and was suddenly illumined by faith, feeling an irresistible urge to claim it for himself. He awoke his fellow-guards and threw his garments in their direction as he hastened, naked, out onto the ice, announcing that he, too, was a Christian.

When morning came and Agricolaos was told about all that had happened, he gave orders that the saints be dragged off the lake and that any still alive be finished off by breaking their legs. Then, in order that there remain no trace of their glorious combat, he ordered that their bodies be burned.

As the bodies were dragged off the ice and piled up on a wagon for transport to the pyre, it was discovered that Meliton, the youngest of the 40, had been set aside and was still alive. Meliton's Christian mother, who had stood on the lakeshore all night sustaining the martyrs with her prayers, had also been given the grace to see the vision of the 40 crowns suspended above the freezing men. She now stalwartly went to retrieve her son's half-frozen body from where it had been set aside. She herself heaved it up on the wagon with the other bodies, saying, "*Do not be deprived of your crown, my dear son. Go join your companions to delight in that eternal light which is now the only thing left me for healing my sorrow and deep grief.*" Then, without a tear, she accompanied the wagon to the pyre, her face filled with joy, knowing that there now flowed into the created world, through the oblation of her son and his 39 companions, that uncreated glory in which lay her only hope.

iii

"True Orthodoxy," which, of course, must always involve the created and its relationship with the uncreated, has been succinctly defined by the great St. Gregory of Sinai as "true knowledge" of the two most basic teachings of Christianity. First is "true knowledge" of the Holy Trinity, which is that God is one God in three equal Persons, Father, Son and Holy Spirit, totally without confusion of Persons and forever existing. Second is "true knowledge" of the two natures of Jesus Christ, He being the Second Person of the Holy Trinity and the only-begotten Son and Logos of the Father who, by the power of the Holy Spirit and the consent of the Virgin Mary, was clothed in her human flesh, perfectly joining together forever in one, single person both His divine and His human natures.

It was, of course, because of their intimacy with this two-natured Person of Jesus Christ that the 40 martyrs suffered torture and death, knowing that in Him was Life, and that that Life was the Light of men. It was, indeed, He whom St. Julitta proclaimed as her "Creator" and her "God who made all things."

One might note in passing, moreover, that Orthodoxy never tires of reiterating these two most basic teachings of "true Orthodoxy" in all she does. Whenever an Orthodox bishop gives his blessing, he holds a two-branched candle stick in one hand, representing the two natures of the one Christ, and in the other a three-branched candle stick, representing the Three Persons of the One God. The congregation before him is blessed as he crosses his arms over the faithful, clutching these two flaming symbols, one in each hand, while invoking God to "*look down from heaven and behold, and visit this vine, and the vineyard which thy right hand hath planted*" (Ps 80:14-15). The triune, uncreated God, Father, Son and Holy Spirit, first revealed to man at the baptism of the two-natured Jesus Christ, is thus regularly invoked by the Orthodox bishop in the midst of his flock, reminding them of Orthodoxy's two most basic mysteries.

Among the Byzantine Orthodox, even the sign of the cross expresses these two basic teachings of the dual nature of Christ and the triune nature of God. The thumb and first two fingers of the right hand are placed together to symbolize the Holy Trinity, while the remaining two fingers lie against the palm, symbolizing the two natures of Christ.

At stake in St. Gregory of Sinai's teaching, of course, is the great truth that "true knowledge" is not at all an intellectual matter, but one that is gained through experience. If one believes that God is good and wants only to serve Him, one will necessarily look upon life differently from one who makes Satan his master. In such a case, servitude to the fallen, created angel renders all pertaining to God objectionable, ridiculous and onerous.

Nor is our present age lacking in persons who knowingly serve the Enemy. Like foolish children, men mock God and try to parody God's works. Boasts of achieving immortality through the definitive cure of old-age and disease vie in the daily press with images of the self-mutilated faces of pop-stars. God and His creation are mocked by man's illusions of self-determination.

But far more pertinent to our consideration of the challenge of the uncreated offered the lover of Christ is the whole question of the dynamism of "right glory" offered man through "true knowledge" of the two natures of Christ and the three Persons of the Holy Trinity. Worshipping Christ as the incarnate Word and Logos and only-begotten Son of the Father, one prays to Him as "Lord," something one can do only through the Holy Spirit, according to St. Paul, as we have already seen. One's basic belief in the uncreated God, therefore, produces a certain dynamism whereby man's created and fallen nature is drawn through prayer actually to participate in the life of the Uncreated, that is in the life of God Himself, Father, Son and Holy Spirit. Focusing one's whole life on such prayer, centered in the heart but ever rising to the Uncreated, is the goal of the lifelong struggle of the great Orthodox ascetics.

Yet Orthodoxy is never elitist in that only the ascetics, or only the monks, or only those officially consecrated to God are expected to seek Him or attempt to partake of Him and His uncreated glory. Baptism is for all who believe, just as the Kingdom, or reign, of the Holy Trinity, into which one is baptized in "putting on Christ," is also for all. "*God is no respecter of persons*" (Acts 10:34), as St. Peter himself concluded.

Not being a "respecter of persons," God, the uncreated Creator, manifests Himself to man as a "*philanthropic God*," a God who is the "*only lover of mankind*," "*the only friend of man*" who "*knoweth our divine longing*," as the Orthodox are wont to proclaim in their liturgical texts. True Orthodoxy allows man to come to know the uncreated Creator on these very intimate terms, since man's calling is that of personally bringing forth the uncreated Logos of God into the world, as did the most holy Theotokos. All men, like her, are called upon to manifest His glory, His beauty and His holiness that others may see Him and glorify God.

iv

St. Paul spoke to the Corinthians of the "*glory of the Father seen in the face of Jesus Christ*" (II Cor 4:6), and, indeed, the full challenge of the mystery of the Church is confronted in the grace of His face. The "*glory of the Father seen in the face of Jesus Christ*" was, in fact, so great that the only-begotten Son of the Father had actually to empty Himself of a large part of it when He became man. By reducing His uncreated, heavenly glory to a humanly bearable glory, that sinful man might not be totally blinded while still being afforded a taste of it on Mount Tabor, the merciful Lord prepared Peter, James and John for the hideousness of His crucifixion, which they would be able to measure against this uncreated glory on the mountain. Unable to bear the full brightness of the vision offered them even in its reduced form, they were still so dazzled by it that they fell on their faces. They were irresistibly drawn to it, moreover, knowing instinctively that it was good to be there in its presence, and they did not want to leave. This aspect of Christ's holy Transfiguration was, of course, echoed in Motovilov's account of St. Seraphim of Sarov's manifestation of the light of the Holy Spirit shown to him. He, too, experienced a profound sense of well-being, as well as being unable fully to bear the sight of it when it first appeared.

Indeed, to participate with Jesus Christ in His glory remains the goal of all who love Him. Yet, this uncreated glory will never belong to those who behold it. Rather, it ever remains the reflection of *His great* holiness, of *His* unlimited uncreated light, the rays of which, as divine energies, emanate from the utterly unspeakable divine essence of Jesus Christ as Uncreated God. This glory, eternally shining forth from the Godhead, is continually transmitted to man through God's divine energies, poured out upon the world. To the extent that sinful man can bear to open himself to such an ineffable reality, to the extent to which man actually thirsts for Him and His glory, is indeed the extent to which man, though a sinner, may, by the Holy Spirit and the prayers of the uncreated Logos for us, come to know the glory He shared with the Father before the world began.

All that can be written on man and on his participation in this ineffable and uncreated glory defies any sort of definitive description, of

69

course. It is, indeed, a part of the profound mystery of the Church that, like the mystery of God Himself, is for us a mystery utterly beyond human concepts. To reduce either God or His Church to a written-out formula confirms man's demonic pride in believing his own human mind to be superior to the greatness of the God-inspired mystery of the relationship between the Uncreated and His creation. Indeed, the mystery of Christ's presence in the poor, the homeless, the destitute and the hopeless is opened only to those who learn how to reach out to Him, hidden as He is in those unlikely images of His uncreated glory. Such is the paradox of the divinely inspired Gospel of Jesus Christ, the glorious, living heritage that ever embodies the mystery of the Church of God.

As Paul Evdokimov wrote, "*It is not the mystery that we understand that is important, but rather the mystery that encloses us,*" and that mystery is indeed the mystery of the Church. It is not a man such as a Pope or Patriarch, but the Holy Spirit Himself who governs the Church. The members of Christ who make up the Church must always be open to the Holy Spirit and to the surprises He reserves for them, rather than preoccupied with their own much-cherished devices.

A mere 50 days after the Resurrection, even as they awaited the descent of the Holy Spirit with its resulting birth of the Church on the day of Pentecost at Jerusalem, which of the Apostles could have foreseen that, before the end of that day, he would be preaching in a foreign tongue unknown to him? It was, moreover, according to the divine will that representatives of the whole international assembly of world Jewry, including many converts to Judaism coming from all over the Roman Empire, be gathered together in Jerusalem for that Pentecost. They thus heard proclaimed, just 50 days after His Resurrection, that Jesus Christ was indeed the Son of God and had been raised from the dead.

Beginning that day, the God of Abraham, Isaac and Jacob, in accord with Jewish prophecies, was indeed to be proclaimed the God of the Gentiles. The Gospel of Christ was, therefore, carried back to the remotest parts of the Empire by those converts coming from that international assembly of fervent Jews who converted and were baptized that day. Christ Himself would thereby become "*a light to lighten the Gentiles and the glory of thy people Israel*" (Lk 2: 32).

THE HEART OF ORTHODOX MYSTERY

It cannot too often be repeated that glory of Pentecost, poured out that day by the Holy Spirit on the assembled disciples, remains the glory of God alone and never the glory of those who are merely His agents in proclaiming it. Paul Evdokimov affirms that the saint always points elsewhere, never to himself. This explains why, perhaps, one repeatedly discovers a certain tension within the Church between those seeking glory in their own schemes of neatly "getting the church in order" and of "shaping things up" so as to prove their success to the world, and those rarer souls who sense, through the Holy Spirit, that perfect organization can never, in itself, suffice in a Church whose glory is found in the Uncreated God and in His glory. Basic to a Christian understanding of God's uncreated glory is the fact that the ultimate glorification of Jesus Christ was truly to be manifested by means of his Passion and Death, the subject He was discussing with Moses and Elijah on Mt. Tabor. Within the divine economy, it was only after He was glorified by His passion, death and burial that He descended to preach to the *"spirits in prison"* (I Ptr 3:19) to emerge triumphant as the Vanquisher of death.

Privy to the uncreated secrets of God, the great Jewish Patriarchs, Moses and Elijah, both saw clearly into the mystery of the Incarnation and, at the Transfiguration, drew nigh to bear witness to what the three disciples themselves would only eventually understand: that the final mystery of creation itself lies in the glorification of the Lamb, *"slain from the foundation of the world"* (Rev 13:8). Suffering and persecuted Orthodox Christians are ever challenged to hold this salutary lesson before them during their often sorrowing pilgrimage on earth.

v

The experiences of those countless Orthodox Christians in the past who embarked on a life lived within the mystery of the Church and who did indeed become holy, in spite of all the perils that threatened this greatest of human vocations, are unanimous in advising those of us who come after them that, without the constant help of God and without the sustenance of the Holy Spirit, one can never even begin to fulfill the enormous potential offered mortal man through a life lived in Jesus Christ.

It is, indeed, a life wherein one must constantly ward off the attacks of the Enemy of the human race. Only when a baptized believer, often after many years and much suffering and anguish concerning his personal struggle, finally arrives at the point where he is willing to pray in complete peace before God, "*I am dust, I am ashes: have mercy upon me,*" can a modest beginning even be made.

The timing of such a confession, and the point at which it is reached, is not important. As we are reminded in the Gospel, the Lord rewards those who come only at the last hour, just as he rewards those who came at the first. The mercy and love of God is never subject to our poor, pathetic human sense of justice or to our paltry sense of "fairness," "equal opportunity" or "political correctness." God, being uncreated, is forever beyond man and man's way of thinking. It is we who are the sheep of *His* pasture. He is not *our* servant. Nor does that priceless intimacy with Him that the saints come to know ever replace the basic awe of fearsome wonder that every believer senses each time he stands before God and lifts his hands to pray "*Our Father...*" as taught by the Lord Himself.

Therefore, when the Psalmist says that he will be satisfied once he knows the "*likeness*" or "*glory*" of God (Ps 16:15), he is actually speaking for every lover of Christ. One may say that man was created with an infinite longing for likeness with the uncreated God, indeed for that glory constituting not only the identity of his Creator, but also the very presence of the Creator in the world. Deprived of that likeness through his fall, man goes about seeking that lost glory in all his earthly endeavors. And, as the Psalmist says, wherever he catches a taste of this lost glory, he is satisfied.

Man's innate longing for glory and for likeness with God can only be derived from the divine longing inspired by the Holy Spirit in every man to return to God from whom, in its fallen state, the human race has drifted away. Glory, that is the "right glory" of Orthodoxy, does manifest the uncreated presence of God in creation. The glory of the Lord shown round about the shepherds on the night of the Lord's birth when the heavenly host drew near, announcing the birth in the flesh and the entry into the fallen world of Jesus Christ, Son of God and Son of the Virgin, just as the glory of God was manifest on Mount Sinai when the Law was given to Moses.

Could there be a greater manifestation of the presence of the Holy Spirit than the manifestation of the glory of the Lord? For in such a

72

manifestation is to be found all the fair beauty of the Lord, all His holiness, all His power and strength. That is why, in willing that men become holy, God also wills that man partake of His glory so that, in fulfillment of the Lord's high priestly prayer, men may themselves see in the saints a reflection of that glory He shared with the Father before the world began.

Alas! Man, however, is so bereft of the glory of the Uncreated that he goes about seeking his glory in illusions about what is of value in the created world, be it money, the glory of this world, success or earthly power. It is not at all by chance that the first of the Ten Commandments, the one determining the keeping of all the other nine, is very simple in its demand: *"Thou shalt have none other gods but me."*

The impact of 18th century idealism, promulgated by the so-called Enlightenment, continues to lead men astray, promising man wondrous things in which to find his glory. Out of this idealism were born, and continue to be born, many utopias, such as Communism or another sort of "new order" promised by the Masonic brotherhood, as well as the so-called "social Gospel," darling to a whole generation of 20th century heterodox Christian scholars. Today's heterodox ecumenical darling is that of Christian unity achieved outside the fullness of truth in Orthodoxy, an illusion that even the Pope, sincerely believing himself to be the "Vicar of Christ on earth," has pathetically thought possible. In the Church of God, however, the Holy Spirit alone can ever be the "Vicar of Christ on earth."

The illusions about man's ability to achieve divine things such as the brotherhood of man is, indeed, a continuation of Enlightenment idealism. All of these fruits of Enlightenment idealism seem to be encompassed, moreover, within the vast embrace of the demonic myth of "progress" that has wrought such havoc in the modern world. It continues to be religiously perpetuated to this day by the empty promises of science and technology.

While man may create the destructive forces equal to a volcanic explosion, by a divine irony he nonetheless remains powerless to control a natural volcanic eruption, or even a hurricane. Where is man's real progress to be detected in this simple truth? His progress is not that of saving himself, but of being able more and more efficiently, more and more hideously, more and more ineluctably to destroy himself and God's creation with him. Nor can he ever prove a match for so-called "natural" cataclysms, which primitive man always rightly viewed as not being unrelated to the will of the gods.

Speaking of man in the mid-19th century, Charles Baudelaire observed that we as a race were destined to perish through that by which we thought we would live. The proof of this is on every side, be it the piling up of nuclear waste, the poisoning of the planet through chemicals, the environmental destruction wrought by the internal combustion engine, or even the simple over-exploitation of natural resources from greed for wealth.

"Scientific progress" has, however, become such a religion that its "development" is financed by governments at preposterous expense while half of the world starves. Yet, the glory of conquering all diseases, and even of conquering death itself, continues to persuade many that no price is too high to pay, even that of begetting children in order to produce a "crop" of embryos for "harvesting" to "advance" wondrous scientific and technological "progress."

The demonic is ever bent not only on the physical destruction of the human race, but also on twisting and profoundly perverting within the human conscience the very image of God as well as anything that might lead man back towards the glory of God. Yet, today, as much as if not more than in the past, the demands of those nebulous illusions offered by scientific and technological progress continue to seduce man. Anyone standing in the way of this satanic enterprise is demonized.

It is not at all impossible that future demonization of Christians for their "anti-progressive" resistance to scientific "progress" could lead to the blind persecution not unlike that of the Christian "atheists" at the time of St. Polycarp. It is not at all impossible that such Christians could be regarded as "enemies of the people," as thousands were, in fact, not only regarded during the French Revolution, but actually guillotined for it.

Regarding human embryos as nothing more than genetic material for research is actually already firmly entrenched in the patterns of our secular 21st century culture. Trying a Christian as a "murderer" of someone denied a transplant because the Christian says "no" to farming human embryos for harvesting as transplant material is hardly outside the realm of possibility in our own times.

vi

Living within the mystery of the church allows us, through the Holy Spirit, to come to terms personally with the mystery that encompasses us, as well as to glimpse the glory of just how it embraces us and all creation. If we truly believe, as taught by the Egyptian contemporary of St. Antony the Great, St. Paphnutios Kephalas, that nothing happens except by God's will or by His permission,[5] then we are obliged to invoke God in regard to all that happens, thereby submitting ourselves and others, and the whole world itself, totally to Him. This is something, of course, that is done liturgically in the Orthodox liturgical admonition "*Let us commend ourselves, and each other, and all our lives to Christ our God.*" Slowly, as one begins to grasp that all that happens does depend either upon God's will or His permission, the mystery of the Church, through the Holy Spirit, allows our focus increasingly to be fixed on God, who sustains not only ourselves, but also all we see around us.

Might one not further observe that the most reliable and indisputable contact we have with our uncreated God, affecting the life of each of us, is, in fact, death itself? Yet, death is also the contact with God against which we react the most violently. We shrink away from it, whether it be in facing our own death or the death of those we know and love. However, if we are believers, we know that death always happens either by God's will or by His permission, for the created world is, in the end, submitted to God's economy, not to the will of man, and certainly not to our own will.

The Orthodox Church, in making "*Christ is risen!*" its supreme and most characteristic cry, attempts, through the all-conquering power of the Holy Spirit made manifest through the Resurrection of Christ, to calm man's perplexity in facing death. Through the Resurrection of Christ, Orthodoxy invites lovers of Christ to subdue the all-encompassing embrace of death, common to the human race, by affirming that death has been swallowed in the unique victory of the Resurrection of Christ. This victory over death is, moreover, experienced in Orthodoxy in an ongoing way

---

[5] This same teaching was much insisted upon by the remarkable Geronitissa Gavrilia of Lemnos (1897-1992) in dealing with her spiritual children.

through the witness borne by the saints who, after their deaths, still show forth the glory of their life in Christ by miracles and wonders.

Life in Christ, or, as the holy Apostle put it, the "*mystery which hath been hid from ages*" (Col 1:26) and which he defines as "*Christ in you*" (Col 1:27), is stronger than what we know as death. "*Christ in us*" is, indeed, life flowing from the uncreated Son and Word of the Father. "*I am come that they might have life, and that they might have it more abundantly* (Jn 10:10)," He continues to assure us in the 21st century.

All Orthodox Christians are, therefore, challenged, within the mystery of the Church, to experience this more abundant life of the Word of God whereby the sinful earthly creature finds his created life being made more complete as it is glorified by the uncreated life of Jesus Christ. By Him "*all things were made*," for He is indeed that uncreated Life that is the "*light of men*" (Jn 1:4).

CHAPTER VI

The Heart of "Christ is in our Midst"

For a lover of Christ to hear the venerable Christian greeting, "*Christ is in our midst!*" with its reply, "*He is, and ever shall be!*" exchanged between believers in the Orthodox Church can prove profoundly moving. This is more particularly true for those lovers of Christ who, after wandering for years in the wastes of heterodox Christianity, where the divinity of Christ seems to be just another academic matter for debate, speculation or even denial, suddenly discover through this exchange that Orthodox Christians have no second thoughts about the immediacy of their intimacy with Christ. To hear proclaimed openly the living presence of the resurrected God-Man, Jesus Christ, here on earth in the 21st century, recognizing that that presence is quite apart from and in addition to His sacramental presence in the Holy Mysteries of consecrated bread and wine, is indeed exhilarating.

Moreover, "*Christ is in our midst!*" with its reply, "*He is, and ever shall be!*" does seem always to exude something of the assurance of the Apostles, of those who braved fire, torture and death to announce the coming of Jesus Christ to the world and His triumph over death. That exchange does, indeed, affirm the conviction that this mighty Conqueror of death is still with us.

Yet, is this not really just a concrete acknowledgement of belief in two promises He made to his disciples? First is His promise, "*Lo, I am with you always, even unto the end of the world*" (Mat 28:20), made to His disciples as He was taken from them into heaven; second is His even more dynamic promise, "*For where two or three are gathered together in my name, there am I in the midst of them*" (Mat 18:20).

The Orthodoxy of the exchange is rooted in what might well be called its "apostolic" intimacy. The holy Apostle's intimacy even with the risen, living Christ never impinged, however, upon the unspeakable awe they had felt before His divinity. St. Peter early on attested to this after the miraculous catch of fish by falling to his knees and declaring, *"Depart from me: for I am a sinful man, O Lord!"* (Lk 5:8).

Such awe could only be inflamed by the descent of the Holy Spirit once they were announcing the Lord's resurrection to the whole world, proclaiming the great mercy bestowed upon it through the revelation of God as Holy Trinity. Had death not been vanquished and hell harrowed by His descending to the dead, as St. Peter attests (I Ptr 3:19)? Yet, their awed reverence before Him and the imperative to make Him known to others were both rooted in their keen conviction concerning His abiding presence on earth.

In the exchange *"Christ is in our midst!"* -- *"He is and ever shall be!"* even the most casual observer is able to sense that the Christ being referred to is something quite other than that nonliving, intellectually conceived Christ, dear to scholars and academics. Indeed, something living and dynamic is implied, something beyond intellectual concepts of Christ and well beyond that commercially exploitable Christ who provides the subject of so many books, debates and sophisticated speculation, art exhibitions, televisions programs and films. In that exchange, it is not merely the historical, biblical, literary or mythic Jesus that is being pursued, but a truly living Person, an abiding Presence, He who is the living God-Man, Jesus Christ, He whose hands and feet still bear the marks of the nail prints, whose side is still marked by the spear wound, and whose head is crowned with scars from the wounds of that fiendishly mocking thorn-crown that was worn for love of the fallen race of man. The uncreated Logos of the Father, the resurrected Christ, is rightly declared by Orthodox Christians to be ever-present on this earth with all those who love Him and call upon Him.

ii

Corrie Ten Boom, that remarkable, dauntless Dutch Protestant believer who, with her equally remarkable sister, was imprisoned by the Nazis for harboring Jews during the German occupation of Holland in World War II, movingly recalls the night following her sister's death in Auschwitz when a rare vacancy had been created in the overcrowded barracks beside her because of her sister's death. When a terrified, solitary woman with Slavic features was unceremoniously thrust into the barracks and abandoned to fend for herself, Corrie Ten Boom caught her eye and, from her double bunk, charitably motioned to the confused and frightened newcomer to come occupy the free place beside her.

Attempts to discover a common language quickly failed, however. Communication was limited to gestures until Corrie Ten Boom, turning towards the newcomer and looking her intently in the face, slowly and very distinctly articulated, as if it were a question, four syllables only: "**JE-SUS CHRIS-TOS?**" The confused newcomer's darkened face immediately became radiant with relief and hope. With a sudden, joyous smile, she crossed herself, then kissed her Dutch benefactor three times on the cheeks.

Corrie Ten Boom had dared seek Jesus Christ in this complete stranger to whom she had offered her dead sister's vacant bunk. She was rewarded by discovering not only that He was indeed in their midst, waiting to be recognized, but that He had sent her a Christian sister with whom she might strive, in mutual love for Him, to bear the endless sufferings and struggles inherent in their situation.

That both women could, in fact, experience His presence by the mere articulation of four syllables designating that "*name which is above every name*" (Phl 2:9) left them with no doubt either about His indeed being in their midst, or that He still could reveal His presence to those who call upon Him, even when surrounded by the most appalling human degradation. In that moment, through the Holy Spirit, all Jesus Christ had meant to each of them in their past life rose up to protect them, revealing to them His uncreated glory in circumstances where normally one would never think of seeking Him. In order "*to receive the King of all,*" as one sings in the words of the Cherubic Hymn, Corrie Ten Boom had fixed her eyes on Him and, in that moment, had "*laid aside all earthly care,*" including the loss of her beloved sister the day before. All personal and selfish misgivings concerning her own unknown, bleak and lonely future, and even her own survival, were subordinated to the fact that Jesus Christ is Lord of the universe. He, ever faithful to His promise, did not fail to prove that He was there with them, even though they were total strangers to one another, one Calvinist and the other undoubtedly Orthodox, uniting them to one another through the power of His mighty Name alone. For the

79

bonds of Christ are always bonds of the living God, woven by the Holy Spirit, and are capable of binding the sinner in peace not only to the Lord, but also to all His Creation.

iii

Intimacy with Christ can, of course, be so easily and successfully imitated by the Evil One. Ever does he seek to destroy the human race by deception, calculatedly employing everything having to do with Christ for his own twisted ends. Demonic illusions may, thus, take on all the outward trappings of an authentic union with Christ in order to deceive thousands into thinking that Christ is in their midst, even when, as in the case of television evangelists, the whiff of commercialism and the disturbing beat of sensational pop music is undeniably present.

It is for this reason that modesty, sobriety and extreme discretion are, through the Holy Spirit, always the marks of an Orthodox Christian's approach to the presence of Christ in our midst. An Orthodox Christian's exhilaration will always tend to be modified by his genuine and very deep awe before the unspeakable mystery of God. Thus, though Orthodox Christians believe that Jesus Christ is always present in our midst, they do tend to shy away from dramatizing this presence by exploiting miracles, as is so ardently done by television evangelists in their pitch for contributions to support their "ministry."

Yet, St. Peter had no money when he and St. John were approached by a beggar, lame from his mother's womb and demanding alms outside the temple in Jerusalem. St. Peter, unable to give him money, said to him, *"Silver and gold have I none; but such as I have give I thee: In the name of Jesus Christ of Nazareth rise up and walk."* (Acts 3:6). The man's cure was even reluctantly admitted by the disquieted and very uneasy temple authorities, who were normally so severe in all their attempts to deny the Resurrection of the living God-Man. The miraculous facts before them challenged their denial, however. Indeed, the influence of the temple had already begun to dissolve, even though the Lord's prophetic statement about its destruction would not finally come to pass until 70 A.D. In that year, Titus's Roman forces would not only destroy the temple, but, in supreme contempt for Jerusalem and the Jewish trouble-makers, plough up the city and render it sterile by sowing it with salt.

In any case, mixing money and miracle-working was hardly invented by modern television evangelists. Charlatans have ever known how to exploit the public's thirst for the unusual, and miracle-working is, indeed, unusual. But exploiting miracles on television is hardly the way of Christ. Was He not ever admonishing people to prudence in speaking of His miracles? Does He not, still today, work quietly through the Holy Spirit within holy Orthodoxy without any need for rock bands or strobe lights?

Indeed, the Holy Spirit, to the glory of the Father, ever bears witness to Jesus Christ as Lord while teaching the Orthodox faithful prudence, modesty and humility as creatures of God. While fully aware of the mighty power of God to work all sorts of miracles, an Orthodox lover of Christ never stakes his faith upon any single wondrous happening, whether to himself or to others. An Orthodox Christian will understand that, within the divine economy of God, however great a personal miracle may be, it is always only a very modest happening when taken in the vast context of the mystery of the Church. It is always of far, far less significance than such great events as the Transfiguration or the Resurrection of Christ, to say nothing of the greatest miracle of all miracles, the Incarnation of God Himself in Jesus Christ. All other miracles become insignificant, paling in comparison with the great mercy given man by a man-loving God in taking on human flesh from the Virgin Mary through the power of the Holy Spirit.

The Incarnation is, humanly speaking, such an "impossible" miracle that, once the power of the Holy Spirit reveals the truth of it to the lover of Christ, no other miracle will pose a problem. After all, the overwhelming truth that "*when God wills, the order of nature is overcome*" lies at the very basis of the Holy Orthodox faith, since Orthodoxy proclaims that the divine Logos of God was, indeed, born of a virgin and made man.

81

iv

Though the experience of Christ's presence in our midst can be powerfully experienced when Orthodox Christians are heard exchanging the greeting *"Christ is in our midst! -- "He is and ever shall be!"* this should in no way impede the lover of Christ from seeking Him in our midst in those less obvious ways in which, He warned us, He can come to us unawares.

In the past century, the God-inspired vocation of Mother Teresa of Calcutta was not only that of recognizing, but of actually serving Christ's presence incarnate in the dying destitute in her midst. Though it was with great depth of focus that Mother Teresa concentrated on one tiny little point of society's horizon, the depth and intensity of her focused concentration embraced all men, as does the grace of God itself. She truly learned to see Him in every dying destitute in all the Calcuttas of the world, as well as in those spiritually destitute, loveless families in Western society. She was, therefore, ever urging all to seek Christ in those around them.

Few of Mother Teresa's dying destitute in Calcutta were Christian at all; rather, they were Hindu, Muslim or other. But did the Lord ever specify that she should limit her search for Him to none but the baptized? Does not His parable of the Good Samaritan profoundly challenge all our man-made restrictions about showing mercy?

In anticipation that many Christians would question how they could have failed to recognize Him in their midst, the Lord portrays them as asking Him on the day of judgment, *"When saw we thee an hungered, or athirst, or a stranger, or naked, or sick, or in prison, and did not minister unto thee?"* (Mat 25:44). He harshly answers, *"Inasmuch as ye did it not to one of the least of these, ye did it not to me"* (Mat 25:45). Thus, when we fail to serve those in need, it is He Himself whom we are failing to recognize as being in our midst.

Christ being in our midst is, therefore, a double-edged sword. It always bears witness to the presence of the Holy Spirit. His presence in our midst is not only a potent and cherished bond between believers who share His presence within themselves by discovering that presence in another, as did Corrie Ten Boom; it is equally the recognition of His presence in those in need with whom bonds may be forged by the power of the Holy Spirit.

Without Christ, such bonds simply would never exist between the world's outcasts and the lovers of Christ.

A healthy balance between these two types of recognition are exemplified in the many accounts of Orthodox saints recounted in the *Orthodox Synaxarion*.[6] There, one finds holy persons who give without asking either the origins or the intentions of the person who receives their charity. Indeed, there are examples of a saint giving double or even triple to someone who had tried to cheat by receiving more in the distribution of goods than he was entitled. Numerous holy people have existed, we read, who systematically refused to keep account of what money they had, leaving it in a place of easy access so that those who needed it might come and take it.

St. Arsenios of Cappadocia (+1922), baptizer of the much-beloved late Elder Paisios (+1994), whose body rests today near St. Arsenios's relics at the women's monastery of Souroti near Thessalonika, was exemplary in seeking to minister to Christ hidden among the unbaptized. St. Arsenios offered his prayers for miraculous cures and healings without distinguishing his faithful Greek parishioners from the many Turkish inhabitants in the same village who also came to him seeking help. St. Arsenios was looked to by everyone in the village to answer for all their needs, both spiritual and physical. Just as the non-Jews were not turned away in approaching Christ when, quite literally, He was in their midst on earth, so also was no one ever turned away by St. Arsenios from the Lord's mercy to sinful men.

Did not the Lord actually admire that Canaanite woman of great faith when He said to her that it was not fair to take the meat of the children of the house of Israel and give it to dogs? And did she not boldly answer Him, "*Truth, Lord: yet the dogs eat of the crumbs which fall from their master's table*" (Matt 15:27)? The Lord proclaimed that this woman's faith was great, and the healing of her daughter, we are told, took place at that very hour.

---

[6] See note 1, p. 7.

V

It is significant that very great saints confound us with their boundless -- one might even say "radical" -- charity. They seem, somehow, to want to stretch all human limits so as to match the boundless mercy of God to the human race. Moreover, for the lover of Christ, the thought that the Lord is ever in our midst in the needy should increasingly become the source of a truly radical humility, since one is forced to recognize one's own impotence. This impotence lies not only in failing always to recognize Him in the needy, but, what is even more disturbing, in responding to this neediness by selling all one has and giving it to the poor and then taking up one's cross to follow Christ.

This evangelical admonition is obviously a sort of absolute, final answer. To this day, it is still recognized and acted upon by those seeking greater intimacy with Christ in the monastic life. But is the person living in the world, therefore, to be considered without hope?

It is here that the mystery of the Church proves so salutary, since, by the ineffable workings of that mystery, and even within the particular challenge of "selling all" implied by it, the Lord in His mercy has not abandoned us who are in the world, nor has He left us without hope of becoming partakers in His Kingdom. There are, of course, cases of married Christians with children who did undertake such a radical departure from the world with their entire family. The grace of their blessedness is not disputed. Yet, the Church of God and its mystery have never been manifested by a two-tiered system among the faithful, such as that found in Manichaeism with its distinction between "ordinary" believers and "perfect" believers.

A Christian Orthodox saint is a saint regardless of his background, rank or state of life. After all, the first person to enter Paradise on Good Friday was not an Orthodox monastic who had sold all, but a thief who, just prior to his death, prayed sincerely, and perhaps even for the first time ever, "*Remember me, O Lord, when thou comest into Thy kingdom*" (Lk 23:42). For, indeed, with God, "*All things are possible to him that believeth*" (Mk 9:23).

For the lover of Christ, recognizing one's inadequacy to right the wrongs of the world is a great grace given by the Holy Spirit, just as, on the other hand, is also sensing God's call to accomplish seemingly impossible things, such as going out and announcing Christ to the world. Yet, the grace of accepting one's inadequacy always serves as a corrective to the modern world's overblown optimism that it is within man's reach to be all-powerful like God Himself and, through economic and social reform and genetic engineering, to banish death and bring Paradise on earth. Such demonic illusions are the confused fruit of the thinking of the 18th century Enlightenment that have succeeded, for the most part, in divorcing Western Christian man from the tremendous mystery of the God of the Bible.

Indeed, man's natural sense of inadequacy is a grace, for thereby man comes to understand himself to be a poor creature. Without this sense of inadequacy, how can man ever learn to pray from the depths of his being, as Orthodox Christians are supposed to pray, repeatedly, every day of his existence, "*O Lord cleanse us from our sins! Master, pardon our iniquities! Holy One, visit and heal our infirmities for thy Name's sake!*" The inadequacy of every man -- monastic or not -- who has "*put on Christ*" in baptism is ever the same. "*Christ is in our midst*" is, however, an ongoing truth that demands man's response, as do all the truths of God. Moses sees the burning bush and is commanded to take off his shoes, for he is on holy ground. Just as the world was judged by Christ's manifestation amongst men, so, too, do we continue to be judged by Him who was incarnate in Jesus Christ and who is still ever-present in our midst.

Yet, Christ's judgment is not something working against the best interests of the human race. Quite to the contrary, what it does is very positive. It takes man, who so often appears to be afloat in the universe without rudder or sail, and directs him towards a specific meaning in life: the recognition of the great intimacy that has been given to him, through the power of the Holy Spirit, to share with the Divine Logos and Word of God in Jesus Christ.

Indeed, the extent to which an Orthodox Christian seeks any identity outside his identity in Christ -- for example, in his ethnic origins or even in his status in the Church -- is the extent to which he is an idolater. After all, being president of a congregation, dressed up in monastic clothing or decked out in the impressive and dazzling trappings of a bishop or patriarch is hardly, in itself, being in Christ. Being in Christ we know to be nothing less than becoming a transmitter of the uncreated light of Tabor, as it was given to St. Seraphim of Sarov to be, sharing this with his disciple. To be clothed with that glory, which is the uncreated light of the uncreated God Himself, is the only final goal in life for any Orthodox Christian. Being clothed in that pristine garment of the Holy Spirit that was bestowed upon every man at his baptism when he was illuminated and truly "*put on Christ*" is, indeed, the final crowning of man as a creature of God.

Though the luminous garment of incorruptibility given in baptism can never be taken away from someone who has "*put on Christ*," it most certainly can be obscured through the sins of the person who wears it. It can even become totally unrecognizable to the world. Joseph Stalin and Adolph Hitler were both baptized Christians. Yet, neither of them is really thought of as a representative of the kingdom of the Holy Trinity. Their kingdom was the kingdom of this world, and they had their reward.

Those who truly love Christ, and who do seek Him and Him alone, are oftentimes given the grace by the Holy Spirit to discover Him in certain holy persons set on their path during their earthly pilgrimage. Indeed, for the lover of Christ to recognize the presence of Christ in those people whose lives have become radiant because of their love for Him is not a negligible aspect of Christian life. Within the mystery of the Church, one always rejoices in such discoveries of the Holy Spirit at work among the race of men, and one is thankful to God for revealing each of them to us. Recognizing saints before they are officially recognized by the Church is a great grace, an Athonite Elder once said to me.

There can be, of course, a certain tension within Orthodoxy between those who are holy and those placed in authority over them, something classically exemplified in the case of St. Nektarios. Those in authority usually feel threatened by the influence of certain spiritual leaders and tension results. This is particularly true if some of their imprudent spiritual children draw up, as it were, a line of defense, quoting their spiritual master as justification for disobedience of their bishop. Bishops naturally tend immediately to suspect that disobedience to their authority is being fomented by the spiritual leader himself, something that is not necessarily the case at all.

There may, of course, be good reason for alarm in cases where the spiritual children, forgetting that it is really Christ alone that they are all trying to serve, seem to set up the spiritual father against all that is not directly associated with him. The temptation to idolatry is ever-lurking for everybody, and the most pious are not exempt.

Such well-meaning but mistaken people obviously fail in their Orthodoxy, since they are not, in fact, seeking Christ, and Christ alone, either in their spiritual father or in their own personal situation. What they really treasure is what they perceive to be their own special, privileged status that they believe has been granted them because of their relationship with their spiritual father. That is the only authority they recognize and one which, they feel, exempts them from any other consideration.

Such blind obedience is the age-old norm in a monastic situation where obedience within the monastery is both essential and of the greatest virtue spiritually. But, as has been shown again and again, trying to apply such monastic discipline of absolute obedience in a non-monastic situation can prove highly problematic, if not actually harmful. When such obedience is applied outside the monastic framework it is very easily used to nurture the pride of the zealot in fostering his desire to shine as a firebrand for Orthodoxy. He, thus, forgets his true role before God as a sorrowing sinner, utterly dependent upon God's mercy for his next breath. Praying, "*I am dust, I am ashes: have mercy upon me!*" is not usually as close to a zealot's heart as is proclaiming, with no small inner satisfaction, that certain brother Orthodox are heretics and not Orthodox at all. He forgets that even "bad" Orthodox are still brethren within the mystery of the Church and that their burden must be borne by the "good" Orthodox soul who prays for them with tears and fear of God, thereby fulfilling the holy Apostle's admonition, "*Bear ye one another's burdens and so fulfill the law of Christ*" (Gal 6:2).

Great saints, such as St. Ireneus of Lyons, struggled with heresies and sincerely wanted to bring the heretics to the "right glory" of the true faith. That disciple of St. Polycarp and direct descendent of the beloved John the Theologian sought to recognize Christ in the heretics, just as Mother Teresa of Calcutta recognized Christ in the dying destitute. Indeed, are heretics not, for the Orthodox lover of Christ, "dying destitutes" spiritually? Their blindness to the "true light" and the "true faith" should ever be a cause of sorrowing supplication before God. Does their blindness not merit the same sort of love and attention that Mother Teresa would have given one of her physically dying destitutes?

To those North American ethnic Orthodox intent upon suppressing all attempts at guaranteeing the availability of Orthodoxy to interested non-Orthodox in their common English language, the half-truth of "Language doesn't matter -- it's all the same," is frequently trotted out to provide a very clever, but insidiously demonic, defense. They thereby pridefully justify their search for a safe refuge in the seeming security of some ethnic group as well as their adamant refusal to be missionaries as commanded by the Lord, going into the world and preaching the Gospel to *all* people and not just those in their own ethnic group.

In the great day of judgment, could there possibly be a greater sin laid at the door of many ethnic Orthodox Churches in North American than that of having failed, so consistently, to show mercy on those unrecognized but spiritually hungry heterodox "little Christs" who came not only to stand at the door of their Orthodox parish, but sometimes even entered as seekers of Christian truth? Unable to be fed spiritually, since they could not understand the language being used, they went away hungry, still thirsting for the water of Life, still naked, because they were never clothed in the Light of Christ Whom they were seeking.

This is not to question, in any way, the absolute necessity of ministering to the non-English-speaking faithful. Ethnic churches have always naturally done this, and its necessity is beyond question. What is questionable, however, (and, one fears, will eventually be reckoned before the great judgment seat of Christ) is that monstrous, idolatrous ethnic pride, arrogantly nurtured by certain members of the North American Orthodox hierarchy, blinding them to the absolute urgency of sharing the fullness of Christ in Orthodoxy with those millions of poor souls born in North America and not of their own culture. For in dealing with Christ and with His fullness, one is never dealing with a matter of culture, but always with a matter of Truth.

Alas! With what congratulatory self-satisfaction do some ethnic clergy grudgingly toss sops to the English-speaking. Repeating the Gospel -- and maybe even the Epistle -- readings in English, or perhaps even going so far as to say the Lord's Prayer or Creed in English after it has been said in the ethnic language are well-established devices aimed at calming the

English-speaking. This would be less serious were it not that, paradoxically, such ethnic clergy at the same time adamantly insist on perpetuating among the ethnic faithful the untruth that those using the ethnic language actually have more than the vaguest possible idea about what is really being said at the altar.

As an example of deliberate self-deception, one might observe that among the Greeks are to be found books of liturgical music where Greek texts are transliterated into Latin letters for the benefit of an English-speaking generation who no longer read Greek letters. Only a person knowing Greek, however, could possibly make sense of all these meaningless syllables in Latin letters. Thus, whereas in reality the largely English-speaking singers are mouthing meaningless syllables with little understanding of what they are singing about, the hierarchy and parish notables can still make themselves believe that the choir is truly singing in Greek and boast that Greek-language worship is happily being perpetuated. Thus do Orthodox Christianity's rich truths become the pawn in a demonic game of the politics of ethnic pride. The Light of Christ is truly kept carefully hidden under an ethnic bush.

The demonic dangerously lurks behind everything that is not God Himself. It certainly consistently manifests itself in the ethnic Orthodox myth that guarding the ethnic language alone will provide a safe bastion for the young against the disintegrating moral influences of the North American world, forgetting that ethnicity is one thing, Jesus Christ quite another. Ethnic pride is a form of idolatry if it hides the presence of Jesus Christ Himself in one's midst and renders Him inaccessible to those non-Orthodox Christians humbly seeking to understand the fullness of Christ in the "right glory" of Orthodoxy's incomparable worship. How can it not be idolatrous to prefer the illusion of ethnic purity to the burning, all-consuming charity of the Spirit of God?

How blessed are those God-fearing ethnic Orthodox souls who humbly, and with fear and trembling, do reach out and do attempt to share the fullness of Christ in Orthodoxy with the heterodox! Because of such rare, God-bearing souls who one day reached out to nurture one's own spiritual hunger and point to the "true light" of the "true faith," lives have been completely changed forever; churches have been founded; vocations have been borne; and Orthodoxy, in being transmitted, has been renewed.

One does well to note the parallel that exists in North America today with the situation of the early apostolic Church. The Church at Jerusalem found itself at odds with St. Paul, who insisted that non-Jews be directly admitted into the Church, whereas the Judaizing party felt that they must first become Jews, submitting to circumcision and other measures of the Law before admission. Indeed, this is not really far removed from what some Orthodox converts can still experience. One may, for example, be told that one must first begin by learning an "Orthodox language," since English has never been an Orthodox language.

Nor is such ill-founded pharisaical elitism by any means dead. I know a former Shiite Muslim whose conversion to Orthodoxy in India entailed not only a total break with his family, but also the threat of death at their hands for having become an "infidel." He escaped to North America only to find himself challenged by North American Greek monks insisting that he "prove" he was a Christian by eating the pork they sadistically set before him.

I have also known an Englishman who entered a North American Russian monastic community with the understanding that he would there be made a priest. As time passed and nothing was said of his ordination, he became uneasy. The following exchange finally illumined him to the truth of his situation.

"Well it turns out that we can never ordain you a priest."

"Why? What has happened? Has something changed?"

"Oh no! Nothing's changed. It's just that you were not baptized Orthodox."

To this the young monk replied, *"Well, if that means I'm not Orthodox, baptize me and make me Orthodox. Then you can ordain me!"*

But the reasoning of the brethren was far more subtle:

"Oh no! You are already Orthodox! There is no question of that. But you were not baptized Orthodox, and that is why we cannot ordain you a priest."

That this young monk left, returned to England and became, in the end, a Greek bishop, need not concern us here. The inalterable fact is that the demonic is always active among those intent upon allowing their ties with Christ to be in any way subservient to their ethnic origins. They are, thereby, often rendered completely blind to the presence of Christ in their midst when He is not identifiable in a familiar, ethnic form.

Christ in our midst may, indeed, take on surprising forms. He may not always be in our midst just as one of the hungry, naked, or imprisoned as in the Gospel. He may just as easily be there in forms that are completely foreign to the carefully preserved ethnicity found in many North American Orthodox churches, speaking only the common language of the country, since he does not understand the ethnic one.

Throughout North America, what are the odds that the Christ appearing in an ethnic parish might be greeted like the fervent young Romanian woman from our university who had arrived in our city just as Great Lent was beginning? She had faithfully found her way to pray every evening during the first week of Lent at the nearest Orthodox Church until, towards the end of the week, a member of the parish, obviously feeling this too-fervent stranger needed to be set straight as to what was what, stopped her as she was leaving and said, "This church is for Greek people!"

Such is the challenge of "*Christ is in our midst*" for all Orthodox Christians.

CHAPTER VII

The Heart of Praying the Divine Liturgy

The power and beauty of Orthodox liturgical worship seems mind-boggling for most observers, Orthodox or not. The music, the vestments, the liturgical movements, to say nothing of the texts used, all combine to make the observer aware that he has entered into a dimension of human life quite different from the one encountered out in the street, at his place of work or even at home. Aesthetes may even treat Orthodox liturgical beauty as an academic subject, failing to grasp that the Divine Liturgy exists only for the purpose of glorifying Almighty God, the uncreated Creator, never just for itself or for man's aesthetic pleasure.

"Liturgy" means "work," and understanding something of the "divine work" of God, as set forth in the Divine Liturgy, is indispensable for revealing the fullness of Christ in Orthodoxy. Indeed, the "work" of the Divine Liturgy is the means whereby man most perfectly expresses the fullness of Christ on earth. In it, the faithful are actually allowed to participate in and become a part of that fullness. All to which Orthodox man aspires, all for which Orthodox man prays, and all to which he lays claim, both in this world and the next, are contained in the Divine Liturgy.

From the beginning of the Church of God, over the course of 2,000 years, Orthodox Christians have unwaveringly held the sacred "*breaking of bread*" (Acts 2:42) on the first day of each week to be the Church's ultimate and most indispensable work. Jesus Christ Himself commanded the offering of bread and wine to be done in remembrance of Him and of His death: "*For as often as ye eat this bread and drink this cup, ye show the Lord's death till he come*" (I Cor 11:26), as the holy Apostle says, who also admonishes the faithful not to forsake their regular, weekly assembly.

This unbroken weekly offering of bread and wine alone continues to justify the existence of the Orthodox Church as the Mystical Body of the Risen Christ. No Ecumenical Council, no assembly of Bishops and Patriarchs, no gathering of the faithful elite, and no banquet of recognition for meritorious service could ever be thought of as either competing with the Divine Liturgy for privilege of place or in any way of being a possible substitute for it. The Protestant mentality whereby one "Sunday service" equals another "Sunday service" (found, for example, in the Anglican Church, where Anglican Matins may happily be substituted for the Eucharist as "the Morning Service" on Sunday) is totally alien to Holy Tradition. It is also utterly foreign to the experience of Orthodoxy's 2,000 years of Christian history.

In speaking of the Divine Liturgy as "work" there is the vital implication that, when man participates in it, he must always make an effort to be an active, rather than passive, praying presence before the altar of God. Many of those filling pews in North American Orthodox parishes, however, do not always seem to be understand this. Indeed, the whole Orthodox idea of "work" when attending the Divine Liturgy entails something far more involved and far more personal than the usual North American, non-Pentecostal Protestant idea of what "going to church" is all about. In such churches, one anticipates sitting comfortably for most of the time, happy for an occasional distraction provided by the choir, the preacher or the singing of hymns.

Unfortunately, many North American Orthodox, in regard to their weekly participation in the Sunday Divine Liturgy, seem happy to opt for something not dissimilar to this North American "going to church" syndrome. Drifting in at the end of Matins, lighting a few candles, and then settling comfortably into a pew, such comfort-seeking worshippers probably even resent being obliged to get to their feet when the priest raises the Gospel Book over the altar and proclaims in a loud voice, *"Blessed is the Kingdom of the Father, and of the Son, and of the Holy Spirit!"*

It is with these words at the Divine Liturgy that the Orthodox Church sets in motion its weekly divine work of interceding before God for the whole world and for the whole of the human race. Strangely enough, the initial invitation to prayer, *"Again and again, in peace let us pray unto the Lord!"* is hardly uttered, however, before most of the congregation discreetly start slipping back down into their pews.

To the outsider, it might seem even that the congregation, by slipping back down into the pews, is quite happy to opt out and leave the priest to "get on with it." How can the man in the pew really be expected to be involved in all those mysterious secret prayers being muttered at the altar? Isn't the main purpose of *his* being there on Sunday morning that of "getting Communion?" If, in fact, he has made an effort to respect the priest's repeated admonition to arrive at the Liturgy before the Gospel is read, he is content, knowing he has made a greater effort than many others in the congregation!

Nor does the prevalent misconception that the congregation is not actually supposed to be involved in praying the litanies always spring just from the congregation alone. Many well-meaning priests -- indeed, even bishops -- have been seen actually to encourage congregational passivity and indifference to the solemn prayer of the Church of God for the world and for the race of men. Such clerics will either turn around and manually gesture for everyone to sit down, or tinkle a little bell from within the altar, or, more dramatically, flick off the little signal lights mounted beside the Royal Doors that, when turned on, bring the congregation to their feet.

Such well-meaning clerics may even register annoyance if some recalcitrant soul remains standing after being signaled to sit down. Are such clerics really unaware that their intervention serves to discourage active participation on the part of the people in their common "divine work" of interceding before Almighty God? If the main activity offered the people is that of passively sitting while the priest carries out the "divine work" on his own, how is it even possible to speak of congregational participation in God's work of praying the Divine Liturgy?

ii

Although the Divine Liturgy is the most familiar of Orthodox services, it is, paradoxically, also the least understood as far as worshippers are concerned. For those who truly pray it, it is indeed the most demanding, for it reveals to the lover of Christ not only the ultimate aim of God's creation within the mystery of the Church, but also the fact that Jesus Christ Himself is the only means whereby we, as sinful men, are enabled to participate in the unspeakable mysteries of Almighty God.

When the priest lifts the Gospel and announces, *"Blessed is the Kingdom of the Father, and of the Son, and of the Holy Spirit!"* the believer is being summoned not only to stand up and pay very prayerful attention, but also to take cognizance of the fact that, in that moment, and there in his own local church, the final, ultimate goal of all creation is being glorified. Participation in it is, moreover, being made available mystically to all those who have put on Christ in baptism. Indeed, all who love Christ are being invited, through the Holy Spirit, to enter into the Kingdom of God, that endless, vast and boundless Kingdom where man will spend eternity either in union with God or in conflict with Him. This explains why a number of the congregation will usually give some sign of recognition that this moment is an unusually solemn one: most worshippers will either simply bow and cross themselves, or touch the floor, or make a full prostration.

In recalling Father John Romanides's observation that the Greek word translated as "kingdom" in English would actually be better translated as "reign," one understands that in the opening proclamation beginning the Divine Liturgy, "*Blessed is the Kingdom of the Father, and of the Son, and of the Holy Spirit!*" the priest is actually extolling the "*reign*" of the Holy Trinity, hailing this reign as "blessed." Whatever may be the many failings and sins of Orthodox Christians in this fallen world, the Orthodox Church itself does unflinchingly bear witness to this reign. She proclaims it at the beginning of every Divine Liturgy, and she glorifies it in the flesh-and-blood witness of her martyrs, confessors and saints. She especially glorifies it, though in a more hidden and secret way, in all those unknown and humble God-fearing Orthodox Christians who, through the Holy Spirit, manifest the reign of the Holy Trinity in their hearts through their unrecognized and obscure everyday life in the world.

How could it be otherwise? The Prince of this world is not Jesus Christ who came to earth to reveal the Holy Trinity as a man-befriending deity to our fallen race. Rather, the true Prince of this world is the Deceiver, the Father of Lies, the Evil One, the Tempter of our first Mother Eve. His temporal reign as Prince of this world, however, is constantly under threat by the eternal reign of the Holy Trinity, proclaimed every time the Divine Liturgy begins in an Orthodox Church.

The believer, for his part, can rejoice that the reign of the Holy Trinity has proven more powerful than the reign of the Prince of this world, more powerful than all the tortures and sufferings, more powerful even than the deaths to which so many Orthodox Christians have been subjected for their faith. The reign of the Holy Trinity can by no means whatsoever be altered, interrupted or effected in any way within the vast, eternal divine economy of God. Even such a cataclysmic happening as the end of the world as we know it can still only be a part of the divine economy, incorporated within the reign of the Holy Trinity, a reign illumined and sustained by the Uncreated God who created us out of nothing and continues to raise us up and redeem us from that nothingness.

As Orthodox Christians, lovers of Christ know in Whom they have hoped and in Whom their faith is fixed. They also know what that blessed Kingdom, of which we are citizens, actually is. Indeed, the lover of Christ knows not only that the Kingdom of the Father, Son and Holy Spirit exists and is a blessed kingdom or reign, but also that in it, all men are free to discover, for themselves, the love and intimacy of that triune God revealed as Holy Trinity by Jesus Christ. The human blood shed by Him, the only-begotten Son and God-Man, has covered them, redeeming them from the snares, deceits and illusions of the Evil One. The Holy Spirit, by whom they have been sealed, sustains and comforts them, both in this life and the next.

The lover of Christ, therefore, relies on a double blessedness in carrying out the "work" of praying the Divine Liturgy: first, the blessedness of the Kingdom -- or Reign -- of the Holy Trinity itself; second, the blessedness of the intimacy with which Orthodox Christians are able, within that Reign, to approach Almighty God, the Creator and Preserver of all things. As sons and daughters who have put on Christ and been sealed with the Heavenly Spirit, Orthodox Christians humbly, yet confidently draw near the Creator of all in offering the Divine Liturgy to Him.

So it is that, in praying the Divine Liturgy, one is never embarking upon a banal, boring activity in the normal, fallen world where not only is man's frustration always the norm, but he is ultimately still led to a frustrating death. Rather, praying the Divine Liturgy becomes, for the lover of Christ, a weekly embarking upon the one true adventure of life itself, an adventure uniting life in a fallen creation to the Source of life, to Him who came that we *might have life more abundantly*" (Jn 10:10). Posited upon the certainty that Christ is risen from the dead and that in Him one never dies, the lover of Christ, in praying the Divine Liturgy, is raised from his paltry, daily preoccupation with mundane things to the contemplation of the uncreated and everlasting joys of heaven itself, where Christ Himself is all in all, where the Father, Son and Holy Spirit, one God, embraces, enlightens and sustains all creation.

iii

The lover of Christ begins his "divine work" at the Divine Liturgy by making his own the words of every petition of the Church articulated by the priest or deacon: "*For the peace that is from above, and for the salvation of our souls, let us pray unto the Lord!*" Thus, it is immediately acknowledged that, within the mystery of the Church, and in spite of the fallen world into which man is plunged at his birth, man's peace and salvation can come only from on high, only from above,[7] from the heavenly reign of the Holy Trinity who descends to dwell personally within man's heart. "*Thy kingdom come, thy will be done, on earth as it is in heaven,*" Christians pray, as taught by the Lord Himself.

The next petition seeks to instill the peace from above into all that exists in the fallen world: "*For the peace of the whole world, the good estate of the holy churches of God, and the union of all men, let us pray unto the Lord!*" The three points in this petition carry the sensitive and praying lover of Christ far. Stretching his imagination, he grasps that the peace he is granted personally by the reign of the Holy Trinity in his own heart could, if spread to the whole world, bring about not only the "*good estate of the holy churches of God,*" but the "*union of all men.*"

---

[7] The translation of the North American Greek Orthodox Archdiocese of this initial petition transmutes "*the peace FROM ABOVE,*" into "*the peace OF GOD,*" thereby annihilating one of man's most basic poetic concepts: heaven is above, a concept hallowed by the Psalmist in writing: "*I will lift up mine eyes unto the hills, from whence cometh my help.*" (Ps 121:1). To annihilate this concept in such an official translation is not only an offense to the Truth embodied in Holy Tradition, but also betrays, alas! a certain arrogance towards English speakers who are supposedly so bereft of spiritual and poetic culture as to be incapable of understanding that "*from above*" in this context could only refer to God.

The third petition becomes even more specific. Rooted in both time and space one prays, *"For this holy house and those who with faith, reverence and fear of God enter therein."* Indeed, at this point there comes into focus all those who, unknown to the praying lover of Christ, have come to pray there in the past, as well as all those countless others still destined to pray to God in that place, to say nothing of those immediately present around him, standing with him and praying at that moment. Through the Holy Spirit, all are mystically joined, all are raised up before God.

There follow further intercessions for the bishop and clergy and for the civil authorities before concluding by remembering the local municipality as well as *"every city and countryside and the faithful who dwell therein."* When this litany of peace for the whole world has been concluded, three antiphons, separated by short litanies, lead up to the Little Entrance.

At the Little Entrance, the angel of the local church is said to enter into the temple as the Christ-proclaiming Gospel Book, borne aloft by the priest and accompanied by light-bearing servers, is solemnly brought out from the altar and then carried to the Royal Doors at the center of the iconostasis. At this point is sung the short Hymn of Entry (*Eisodikon*), which, except on special feasts, is simply an invitation to bow down before Christ: *"O come, let us worship and bow down unto Christ!"* Unfortunately, this weekly invitation often seems to spark only mediocre response from most of the congregation.

The Little Entrance completed, and the priest and servers having returned behind the iconostasis, special hymns (*Troparia*) proper for that day and for that particular parish are sung while the priest prays the prayer of the Thrice-holy hymn (*Trisagion*) in preparation for the solemn singing of that key text. In this prayer, the priest beseeches God to receive *"even from the mouth of us sinners the Thrice-holy hymn and visit us with thy goodness."*

> *Pardon us every transgression both voluntary and involuntary, sanctify our souls and bodies; and grant us to serve thee in holiness all the days of our life, through the intercessions of the holy Theotokos and of all the saints,*

> *who from the beginning of the world have been well-pleasing to thee.*

This last statement, though seldom heard, draws us immediately out of ourselves, joining us to the wondrous, cosmic dimension of all those who have loved and served God from the beginning of time, asking that, with them, we may also be pleasing to Him. In this text evoking "*the beginning of the world*," the cosmic dimensions attached to the adventure of praying the Divine Liturgy become both explicit and very specific.

In spite of the Trisagion's familiar presence at the beginning and end of formal Orthodox prayers, there is, nonetheless, a sort of ultimate and absolute dimension attached to it. It is not only the text sung on Good Friday as the bier of the Lord is carried in procession around the church three times, but also the text sung as the body of an Orthodox Christian is borne to the grave. Unfailingly, the created is brought before the face of the Uncreated by death.

Certainly, no text more profoundly traces the distance between the fallen race of man -- the creature -- and the man-loving, uncreated God of Orthodoxy than the Trisagion. Its text succinctly proclaims the absolute *otherness* of the being of God when compared with the created order of mortal man who, unlike God, is by nature not holy, mighty, or immortal. Basically, the Trisagion invokes mercy from Him who alone possesses these divine characteristics: "*Holy God! Holy Mighty! Holy Immortal! Have mercy upon us!*"

iv

Said to be sung by the angels before the face of God, the Trisagion, when formally sung by the choir and congregation prior to the Epistle and Gospel, does constitute a sort of high point for the whole first part of the Divine Liturgy. Indeed, in Greek usage, after its third singing, there is even a chanted admonition by the priest to sing it a fourth time with still greater strength!

Though there are special occasions during the liturgical year when other texts replace the formal singing of the Trisagion at the Divine

Liturgy, these are few. This text is actually considered such a basic element of the Divine Liturgy that the Cherubic Hymn refers to the fact that the congregation mystically represents the Cherubim simply by singing its holy text. The importance of the "divine work" they are engaged in is thus recalled to the worshippers. Indeed, the Trisagion-singing congregation, there in their local parish, are said mystically to be emulating, on earth, the Cherubim in heaven who unceasingly and uninterruptedly sing the same text before the face of God. What is of interest in regard to the congregational singing of the Trisagion at this point is that it serves to focus worshippers' minds on the uncreated characteristics of God by which He is so radically separate from them and from their created order: His holiness, His might and His immortality. We recognize Him for Who He is. We try to grasp how His nature is so diametrically opposed to our own poor, fallen, created nature as we, firmly rooted on earth, stand before Him who is holy, mighty and immortal and pray for mercy.

The implication that we actually resemble the Cherubim merely by proclaiming that God is so radically different from ourselves, moreover, encourages us to taste and see how good the Lord is. In consciously recognizing Him as holy, mighty and immortal, our minds are borne upwards towards something higher, something above, something far beyond the limitations of our fallen, mortal state.

The Trisagion is, therefore, a sort of summons prior to the reading of the Epistle and Gospel bidding us to incline our necks, our hearts and our souls before that uncreated Light of the Holy Trinity pouring forth from the face of Almighty God and continuously hymned by the Cherubim. Indeed, the real work involved here is not just that of bowing our heads and necks before almighty God, but, even more, of opening our hearts to receive Him as He is. Inwardly, we seek to embrace Him and strive to acquire, through the divine grace of the Holy Spirit, His holiness, His might, and His immortality as we humbly bow before Him, cross ourselves, and sing repeatedly: "*Holy God! Holy Mighty! Holy immortal! Have mercy upon us!*" Thus is one more intimately open to receiving both the teaching of the holy Apostle contained in the Epistle and the life-giving words of the Gospel of Christ that will follow.

V

Although the prayer read prior to the proclamation of the Holy Gospel is applicable to all present, it is seldom heard unless the priest, bold in the Holy Spirit, insists on sharing the "secrets" of what he is saying at the altar with the praying congregation. The faithful whose priest does try to initiate them into the divine mysteries, quietly encouraging them at each Divine Liturgy to enter with him more and more intimately into the holy of holies as he prays, can truly call itself blessed by God.

Illumine our hearts, O Master who lovest mankind, with the pure light of thy divine knowledge, and open the eyes of our mind to the understanding of thy gospel teachings; implant in us also the fear of thy blessed commandments, that trampling down all carnal desires, we may enter upon a spiritual manner of living, both thinking and doing such things as are well-pleasing unto thee.

The emphasis here is of importance, for in seeking to trample down "*all carnal desires*" one is trying to become, like St. Alexis, a "man of God." Developing a taste for the spiritual aspect of human existence is, in fact, the only means whereby one may understand the mysteries of the Gospel of Christ. Indeed, how can a non-spiritual man hope to grasp even the most basic implications of the Parables?

The absolute necessity of approaching God as a *spiritual* man rather than as a *carnal* one is, moreover, echoed once more in the priest's prayer of the Cherubic Hymn, beginning with the lines:

No one who is bound with the desires and pleasures of the flesh is worthy to approach or to draw nigh or to serve thee, O King of glory, for to serve thee is a great and fearful thing, even to the heavenly powers. Nevertheless through thine unspeakable and boundless love towards mankind thou didst become man, yet without change or alteration, and as Master of all did take the name of our

101

High Priest and delivered unto us the ministry of this liturgic and bloodless sacrifice.

Thus, within the mystery of the Church, the ministry of the Uncreated has been entrusted to the created, in this instance the priest who is praying. The words of the closing lines of this prayer are particularly potent in their implications:

For I draw near unto thee. Turn not thy face from me, neither cast me out from among thy servants, but vouchsafe that these gifts may be offered unto thee by me, thy sinful and unworthy servant; for thou thyself art he that offereth and is offered, that accepteth and is distributed, O Christ our God [...].

Christ is indeed He that offers and He that is offered, He being both priest and victim, like St. Polycarp who, filled with the Holy Spirit and knowing Christ to be abiding in Him, laid aside his outer garments and shoes to mount the pyre as a victim of holocaust.

So it is that, at each Divine Liturgy, we even today, in spite of our sins and to the extent that we are truly joined to Him and abiding in Him and He in us, are both invited and enabled by the Holy Spirit to become, with Christ, both priests and victims in His divine Eucharistic oblation, losing ourselves in Him Who, in that oblation, becomes all in all for us, as for all creation. Thus, while the choir and people are singing the text of the Cherubic Hymn, *"Let us lay aside all earthly care that we may receive the King of all,"* the text actually being prayed at the altar by the priest does clearly imply an actual fusion between the congregation receiving Him in Holy Communion on the one hand and, on the other and at the same time, also of being offered up with Him to the extent that we have indeed become one with Him, that is, wholly joined to Him, *"hid with Christ in God"* (Col 3:3) as the Apostle writes.

As one moves forward to the Holy Anaphora, or Oblation, the "work" of the praying people is more than ever strikingly implied by the invitation, *"Let us love one another, that with one accord we may confess,"* completed by the choir's answer, *"Father, Son and Holy Spirit: the Trinity, one in essence and undivided.*" The "divine work" of loving one another is, therefore, plainly viewed as absolutely indispensable to being enabled to confess the truth of the Trinity, which is about to be done in the recitation of the Creed.

The faith in the Trinity as expressed in the Creed having been confessed in a unity of love for one another, the people are immediately admonished to "*stand aright*" and "*with fear*" that they, with the priest, may "*offer the holy oblation in peace.*" The response of the choir, "*A mercy of peace, a sacrifice of praise,*" anticipates the mystical fusion about to take place between the "peace from above," prayed for in the first petition of the first litany, with the Eucharistic "sacrifice of praise" now about to be offered. Indeed, it is only because we have both received and entered into that spiritual and heavenly peace of the Uncreated God that we are enabled to offer back to Him the sacrifice of Christ, the sacrifice of Him in Whom we, as all creation, alone truly discover not only our purpose and our true identity, but "*our peace*" (Eph 2:24).

Thus does "*a mercy of peace*" become also "*a sacrifice of praise,*" to the extent that those present are truly praying in peace and genuinely attempting, by abiding in Him, to offer themselves to the Father. For in the Lord's great mercy we are allowed to be in Jesus Christ and discover our true identity as being found in Him alone to the extent that we offer ourselves with Him in the Eucharistic sacrifice, with fear of God, with faith, and with love for one another through the Holy Spirit. The sacrifice of the Holy Mysteries is not something reserved only for the clergy, but has always been intended for the baptized people of God that, through the Holy Spirit, they may join in the Lord's oblation and sanctify the world through Him to the glory of God the Father.

At this point, the priest issues the invitation, "*Let us lift up our hearts!*" to which the choir answers affirmatively, "*We lift them up unto the Lord!*" This is followed by a second invitation, "*Let us give thanks unto the Lord!*" at which point certain worshippers may make a sign of deep reverence while the response, "*It is meet and right!*" is sung. This is followed by the earthly congregation joining with the cherubim and seraphim singing before God the triumphal hymn, "*Holy! Holy! Holy! Lord of Sabaoth; heaven and earth are full of thy glory: Hosanna in the highest!*

Blessed is He that cometh in the Name of the Lord! Hosanna in the highest!"

The words by which the Lord first instituted the consecration of bread and wine to be His immaculate Body and His precious Blood are next heard and draw a fervent "*Amen*" from the choir just before that most solemn of declarations bursts forth from the priest: "*Thine own, of thine own, we offer unto thee, in behalf of all, and for all!*"

As we have already observed, these words do imply that, in offering the Lord Himself to Himself, we are also offered with Him to the extent that we are truly abiding in Him and He in us. Surely there is no moment of the Divine Liturgy more potent with possibilities than this one for inwardly participating with heart and soul and all one's being in so many dimensions in the "divine work" being carried out at the altar. For the prayerful lover of Christ, nothing less than the whole of the cosmos itself is being implied, in that the offering is being made "*on behalf of all, and for all.*" Moreover, the true lover of Christ will understand himself to be an integral part of that offering both by virtue of being in Christ himself and by virtue of having Christ abiding in Him through the Holy Spirit. Has he not indeed "*put on Christ*" in baptism?

One can understand why one may see the whole congregation fall to its knees at this so solemn declaration. Should such a declaration not indeed inspire a response of absolute, total prostration, the whole congregation bowed humbly before God with faces to the ground? One is, indeed, caught up in the ineffable mystery of the timeless, Uncreated God, Who deigns in this moment in earthly time to be joined in a mystical, bloodless sacrifice in which all who love him are allowed to be incorporated and become co-participants.

Could a sharper contrast to the sacrifices once offered daily in the temple of Jerusalem, with their stench of burning flesh and perpetual streams of animal blood, be imagined than this all-inclusive, cosmic and bloodless mystical sacrifice? Moreover, it is an offering for the whole of creation, which Orthodox Christians were commanded by the Lord to offer until He comes again. All who have loved God from the beginning of creation are mystically joined before the face of God. For the Logos-Creator-Redeemer-Lamb, slain from the foundation of the world, in that moment and in union with His unique offering made on Calvary once and for all as the Great High Priest, offers Himself to Himself through the "divine work" of the Orthodox Church.

Indeed, at the end of the consecration, after recalling the ever-blessed memory of the most holy Theotokos and having sung her glorification, the priest remembers his Orthodox bishop. To this essential commemoration -- for the Church of God is rooted in the reality of human history as also in historic fact -- the choir should answer with abounding inclusiveness, *"For all men, and for all things!"* Unfortunately, *"For all men, and for all things!"* is often mistranslated to give the very weak line, *"And for all mankind!"* or *"For each and every Orthodox Christian!"* for example. Thus, the whole cosmic sweep of that all-inclusive petition, which is intended as the final commemoration as the Church of God completes her Holy Oblation offered for the life of the world, is considerably diminished and watered down.

vi

The reception of the holy Body and Blood of the Lord is, therefore, something quite different from what is thought of in the popular mind as "getting Communion." The actual physical ingestion of the Holy Mysteries into our bodies is the sealing -- as it were, the crowning and confirmation -- of all that has already gone on in the "divine work" carried out by the praying lover of Christ. Such a lover of Christ, abiding in Christ, has, through the Holy Spirit, offered himself up with Christ *"on behalf of all and for all"* so that, in approaching the holy chalice, it is no longer he who lives, but Christ who lives in Him. His heart has been made ready by turning away from carnal things to spiritual things and, in the Holy Spirit, by loving his brethren and confessing with them the right glory of God as Holy Trinity.

While it is obvious that the plentitude of being forever in Christ can be fully achieved only after much suffering in this life and can be lived out fully and in complete perfection only in the next life, so great is the Lord's mercy to sinful man that He allows man, briefly, in the Eucharistic oblation of Christ, to *"taste and see"* (Ps 34:8) just what being totally in Christ can mean.

105

Thus, one comes to understand that praying the Divine Liturgy is indeed "divine work." Never can it be for the lover of Christ just a boring, passive prelude to being able to go forward finally to "take Communion" when the priest brings out the holy chalice. How blessed are those who crown their divine work of praying the Divine Liturgy with an extreme reverence in approaching the holy chalice! By the grace of God, it is not unknown among the Orthodox for one praying soul, through the Holy Spirit, to inspire other souls around him to pray with greater fervor. So it is also that reverence shown in approaching the holy chalice may likewise inspire a greater reverence in others. How blessed is that soul who, with tearful awe can, in the Holy Spirit, rightly confess the presence of the Lord in the Holy Mysteries by whispering the cry of the no-longer doubting Thomas: "*My Lord and my God!*" (Jn 20:28).

Such a supreme opportunity for confession and encounter is offered the true lover of Christ whenever he, through the Holy Spirit, with faith and love and fear of God, draws near the holy chalice containing the Bread of Life, thereby crowning his "divine work" of praying the Divine Liturgy. Streams of Living Water, which the Lord said "*shall be in him a well of water springing up into everlasting life*" (Jn 4:14), flow to the lover of Christ from that sacred cup, for it is the Uncreated God Himself that it contains.

As a lowly member of the Mystical Body of Christ, the pious communicant is, in that moment and through the fullness of Christ, at one with all those who since the beginning of time have glorified God. For Jesus Christ, being the Logos of God from the beginning, is, as the holy Apostle wrote and as the Orthodox Church proclaims, "*all, and in all*" (Col 3:13). Before Him, the communicant bows in tearful worship as did the blessed Apostle Thomas when he confessed, his heart full of awe and humility, "*My Lord and my God!*" (Jn 20:28).

Such a confession is, indeed, the only response possible in answer to the ongoing challenge offered a lover of Christ in praying the Divine Liturgy.

CHAPTER VIII

The Heart of the Order of Melchizedek

For an Orthodox Christian, there can be no sadder, more pathetic or depressing image of Christian pilgrims to the Holy Land than that seen from time to time on fundamentalist religious television programs, where young fundamentalist Christians attempt to celebrate ancient Jewish feasts in Jerusalem. Failing to understand that Judaism has been completely superseded by the coming of Jesus Christ, these enthusiastic young people stage rather absurd rituals in which processions, dancing and singing in the open air are featured.

Since those taking part in these spectacles do seem to be, for the most part, Americans, it is perhaps only natural that America's penchant for Hollywood spectacles is evident. Overly exuberant young women and a certain number of exuberant young men, all clad in long robe-like dresses and wearing Eastern-style jewelry, wave tambourines and branches, dancing and singing in the vicinity of Jerusalem in seemingly joyous, but obviously contrived abandonment. They are supposedly honoring some Jewish festival utterly unknown to most of the viewers.

There can be no doubt that the majority of these enthusiastic participants are pursuing a misguided attempt at union with the Jewish roots of Christianity. Perhaps they think that this spectacle will provide them with greater authenticity in their own deep Christian commitment? What is pathetic is that, in good faith, they are genuinely seeking to establish a closer bond with Christ Himself, undoubtedly reasoning that He too, like them, would once have been dancing and celebrating as a Jew in Jerusalem.

True to their Protestant roots, such fundamentalist Christians, with their heterodoxy and fundamentalist American television time, blithely skip over all that has transpired since the time of Jesus. They attempt, as Protestantism is ever wont to do, to "go back" to more primitive times when everything had not yet become "corrupted," as they perceive the present time to be. Knowing that Christianity came out of Judaism, they attempt to make of that fact all they can. The limit of their own imagination is the only limit they will recognize.

Historically speaking, they fail completely to understand that the Church of God, as the Orthodox Church has ever been and still is, is not something to be fashioned by man and man's intellectual prejudices. Rather, it has been fashioned throughout 2,000 of human history by the working of the Holy Spirit in the hearts of men. For the Church of Jesus Christ has to be a continuing, living, ongoing reality against which He Himself has promised that the gates of hell shall not prevail.

Indeed, Protestantism, a product of Renaissance humanism, has ever tended to approach the mystery of the church through human intellect alone. For such man-centered Protestant thinking, nothing can be good unless man is able to understand it, attach a label to it, and classify it. The many lessons to be drawn from the vast history of Christianity are not likely to tempt the individual who believes in the sacredness of his own reasoning, enlightened by his own reading of the Bible. Thereby he believes it possible for him to create the Church of God itself. What they do not understand they view as threatening, which explains much of fundamentalism's deep suspicion of Orthodoxy.

Indeed, Orthodoxy fails to appeal to Protestants in many cases simply because Orthodoxy demands that one approach the relationship with God as something spiritual and mysterious, not something controllable by man's intellect alone. Worship in "*spirit and in truth*" (Jn 4:23) always implies something beyond intellectual formulae, since the Uncreated God, incarnate in Jesus Christ, is a living God and can never be grasped unless one is endowed with a burning desire to participate, through the Holy Spirit, in the divine life of Jesus Christ Himself and in His uncreated glory, loving Him that He may, with the Father, come and take up His abode with him (Jn 14:23).

In any case, Middle Eastern costumes, glittering necklaces and jangling tambourines do not elucidate the true ties existing between Jesus of Nazareth and Christianity today. Furthermore, they do not in any way lead one to understand why, in the Orthodox Church, one finds the faithful, without costumes, necklaces or tambourines, quietly and confidently still exchanging the kiss of peace with the words, "*Christ is in our midst!*"--"*He is and ever shall be!*" as has been done since Apostolic times.

THE HEART OF ORTHODOX MYSTERY

The frantic efforts of the heterodox to authenticate their own humanistic approach to Christianity by attempting to recreate Jewish ceremonies of the distant past appears to be something peculiar to American Protestantism. Well might one ask, "And where are the real Jews in such ceremonies?" Such attempts are as pathetically lacking in historical focus as are the claims of the Roman Catholic Church to have jurisdiction in the Holy Land, to say nothing of Rome's claims of infallible and universal jurisdiction over all Christians belonging to the Church of God.

ii

It is only natural, of course, that all Christians look upon Judaism as the one, unique religion making possible the Incarnation of God in Jesus Christ who, by the power of the Holy Spirit, took flesh from the ever-Virgin Godbirthgiver, fulfilling prophecy after prophecy in Judaism that foretold His sacrificial and redemptive mission in coming into the world. Within the mystery of the divine economy, moreover, it was through the divinely chosen people, the Jews, that Almighty God, in the fullness of time, did reveal Himself as Holy Trinity through the Incarnation of Jesus Christ.

The beginning of the pact between God and the Jews started, of course, with the great patriarch Abraham, whose blind and absolute faith set the pattern to be pursued by lovers of God to this day. In this matter of blind faith there is absolutely no break, no rupture and no compromise over the centuries. St. Paul himself holds up the example of the faith of Abraham as the prototype for Christian believers in his own day, something that is still universally accepted.

Whatever it may be with the covenant made between God and Abraham, and whatever it may be with that great patriarch's blind faith in obeying God without question, the worship of the one true God still did not actually begin with Abraham. Sacrifices had been offered to God from the time of Cain and Abel; and we know that sacrifice was offered to God by Noah after the flood. Abraham was, thus, the father of a race whose relationship with God was far older than Abraham.

109

St. Paul, who views Jesus Christ as *"a merciful and faithful high priest in things pertaining to God, to make reconciliation for the sins of the people"* (Heb 2:17), nonetheless meticulously separates the eternal priesthood of Christ from that hereditary Aaronic priesthood that presided over the temple devotions of his day. What is of particular importance for Christians, however, is that though the Jewish priesthood had come from the descendants of Abraham, or, more specifically, from Aaron and the tribe of Levi, this priesthood was only for a given period and for a given people. It forever ended once the Gospel of Jesus Christ had been proclaimed: *"But when that which is perfect is come, then that which is in part shall be done away"* (I Cor 13.10).

St. Paul takes pains to point out that, prior to God's pact with Abraham, there did exist the mysterious priesthood of Melchizedek. Melchizedek was, St. Paul affirms, both the "King of righteousness" as well as the "King of Salem," which, being interpreted, means "King of Peace." It was before this King of "righteousness and peace" that Abraham, after his victory in battle, bowed down paying tithes of tribute, thereby recognizing him as a true priest of the true God of righteousness and peace Whom Abraham served.

This mysterious pre-Abrahamic priesthood was forever hallowed by the Psalmist in announcing, *"Thou art a priest forever by the order of Melchizedek"* (Ps 110:4), words St. Paul took as a prophecy foretelling the eternal priesthood of Jesus Christ Himself (Heb 6:20 - 10:21). St. Paul wished to explain to the Jews, who violently resisted the fact that Jesus Christ was the Son of God, how it was possible that a normally accepted priority in matters of religion, such as that of the Aaronic priesthood, which prior to Jesus Christ had actually been the only "valid" one (even though it had been interrupted by conquests of Jerusalem), could be superseded and replaced by other priorities, priorities that were also the fulfillment of prophesies.

Faced with the refusal by so many of his brother Jews to accept Jesus Christ as the crowning of the divine covenant made not only between God and the Jews, but between God and creation itself, St. Paul argued that the Aaronic priesthood, instituted under Moses and still in effect in Jerusalem in his day, had come to an end with the coming of Jesus Christ. He Who is indeed the true King of righteousness and of peace, Jesus Christ, through His Passion, Death and Resurrection, had inaugurated a priesthood that was not at all dependent upon the priesthood of Aaron. Be that as it may, it was the temple cult, carried out by the priesthood of Aaron, that did provide the Apostle with those glorious images he uses to explain the sacrifice and expiation for the world fulfilled by the crucifixion of Christ. For the priesthood of Christ was a truer priesthood than that of the temple priests in Jerusalem, since this priesthood, St. Paul argues, "*is made, not after the law of a carnal commandment, but after the power of an endless life*" (Heb 7:16). Indeed, Jesus Christ lives forever and is not subject to that perennial mortality plaguing not only the Aaronic priesthood, but indeed all other mortal priesthoods. Jesus Christ, moreover, had conquered death through his Passion, Death and descent into Hell. What the older Aaronic high priest ceremonially accomplished once yearly when he entered into the second tabernacle with blood "*which he offered for himself, and for the errors of the people*" (Heb 9:7), Jesus Christ Himself, once and for all eternity, "*neither by the blood of goats and calves, but by his own blood he entered in once into the holy place, having obtained eternal redemption for us*" (Heb 9:12). St. Paul's argument thus carries us to the very heart of the mystery of the oblation of Christ in which our hope as Christians is fixed.

> *For if the blood of bulls and of goats, and the ashes of an heifer sprinkling the unclean, sanctifieth to the purifying of the flesh: how much more shall the blood of Christ, who through the eternal Spirit offered himself without spot to God, purge your conscience from dead works to serve the living God?* (Heb 9:13-14)

St. Paul's chief argument is that the very carnal priesthood of Aaron was of a lesser spiritual order than the priesthood of Melchizedek, which it followed. The priesthood of Melchizedec, indeed, foreshadowed the eternal, cosmic priesthood of Christ, who, within the divine economy, fulfilled all things. Only through the experience of the sons of Abraham, however, could the world be prepared for the coming of the Christ. That Abraham paid a tithe to Melchizedek, St. Paul insists, in any case proves the superiority of the earlier priesthood, now restored and fulfilled in Jesus Christ.

All of this, of course, changes nothing in regard to the exemplary blind faith of Abraham in his covenant with God. It was this faith alone that caused him not only to leave his own country to follow God's command, but also to go on to establish a race that, by staying faithful to its origins in Abraham, would, in worshipping the one true God served by Melchizedek, develop its own priesthood and the cult of animal sacrifice. The true fulfillment of this race of Abraham with its cult of animal sacrifice, however, was to be realized only in this new, Christocentric priesthood, incarnate, both in this world and the next, in Jesus Christ. He is, after all, the Second Person of the Holy Trinity, the eternal Son and Logos of God, begotten of His Father before all ages, incarnate by the Holy spirit and the virgin Mary: "*God of God; Light of Light; very God of very God; begotten, not made.*" This new and final priesthood inaugurated by Jesus Christ and attaching itself to the pre-Abrahamic priesthood of Melchizedek would, thus, replace the older priesthood of the Jewish temple.

In fact, St. Paul argues that, since "*our Lord sprang out of Judah: of which tribe Moses spake nothing concerning priesthood*" (Heb 7:14), this itself is a sign that the older Aaronic priesthood had no further purpose after His coming. Indeed, according to the older Jewish order, Jesus Christ could never possibly have been a priest to begin with since He was not of the priestly tribe of Levi, but of the tribe of Judah. The prophecy cited by the scribes in reply to the Wise Men's inquiry about where Christ should be born actually announces that He Who was to be born in Bethlehem was destined to become the ruler of God's people, Israel:

> *And thou Bethlehem, in the land of Judah,*
> *art not the least among the princes of*
> *Judah: for out of thee shall come a*
> *Governor, that shall rule my people Israel*
> (Mat 2:6).

What is obviously being referred to here had to be the people of the new Israel, which is the Church of God, the Bride of Christ. Her governor has ever been Jesus Christ.

112

iii

Ancient Judaism, which provided Christianity with a solid parentage in which God had repeatedly revealed His nature, also provided man with numerous examples by which man's stance, conduct and comportment might be measured in relationship with the living God. *"Put off thy shoes from off thy feet, for the place whereon thou standest is holy ground"* (Ex 3:5), were words uttered by the angel from the burning bush to Moses when he, the unworthy, encountered God in that theophany. The encounters with God in the Old Testament are, moreover, always filled with awe and true fear of God's great power and majesty.

The doubts and hesitations, the dread and fear of God, the attempts to bypass God: all these things are described again and again in the Old Testament experience of God and are hallowed in the experience of God shown by the psalmist. They are, moreover, still lived out by Christians just as they were lived out by the Old Testament prophets and holy men of God, for God Himself in Jesus Christ does not change and is forever the same (Heb 13:8).

What seems to be different, however, in our attempts today to encounter the presence of that same dread and awesome God, is that, because of Jesus Christ, we are now obliged to come to terms with the *kenosis* of the Word of God, that is, the unsurpassed self-humiliation necessary for Him to be able to manifest Himself to us. We, who by the grace of the Incarnation and by the grace of our baptism are joined in a mystical way to Jesus Christ Himself, are thereby called upon -- summoned -- to partake of that absolute humility of His *kenosis* by which He emptied Himself of the glory He shared with the Father from before the worlds. Learning to partake of His *kenosis*, so freely offered to us, is vital if we are also to participate in His uncreated glory. The great difference is that what we must strive to empty ourselves of is not at all the great uncreated glory that is eternally His in His Godhead, but rather all that is contrary to that glory. We must, in fact, empty ourselves of all that is not God, thereby making room for Him to enter into our hearts and souls. Only by emptying ourselves of all that is not His glory can we ourselves strive to rise towards Him Who is ever descending to us through the Holy Spirit and His ongoing *kenosis*, so that we, by His grace, may partake of His glory.

113

Indeed, *"grace and truth came by Jesus Christ"* (Jn 1:17), as the Beloved Disciple affirms, a grace and truth unknown in Judaism. The final crowning of the fullness of the revelation of the God of Abraham, Isaac and Jacob was, within the Divine Economy, to be given man in Jesus Christ alone through that divine *kenosis* by which He came down to man.

Christian man's make-up in the 21st century, moreover, does prove uncannily faithful to the experience of the Old Testament patriarchs and prophets. It has in no way changed. Modern Christians are still fearsome and hesitant. They are still not particularly eager to admit their fundamental helplessness before God. Modern man still longs to find a hiding place where he can be alone and away from God's all-weighing presence, away from His all-seeing eye. However, though the lives of such struggling and fearsome Christians are so similar to the lives of the ancient patriarchs, St. Paul maintains that Christians, nonetheless, have been accorded a special grace that all the Old Testament witnesses to the living God were never accorded. Indeed, the holy Apostle insists, as we have already observed, that all those who came before Christians were not to be made perfect (Heb 11: 34-40) without those who have been shown the fullness of the revelation of God in the Holy Trinity through the Incarnation of Jesus Christ.

iv

What then is so radically different from the Aaronic priesthood and that priesthood of Melchizedek, held up for our admiration by St. Paul? It seems to be that, whereas the Aaronic priesthood was dependent upon birth and race, the older priesthood of Melchizedek, according to St. Paul, partook of a more timeless quality, defined neither by birth nor by race. Thus, whereas Jesus Christ could only have been born a Jew according to the divine economy, His priesthood was freed from all the usual restraints of the Hebraic priesthood. Was this not, in fact, something foreshadowed by the most holy Godbirthgiver herself being freed from all the usual restraints against women when, as a child, she not only penetrated the temple, but was introduced into the Holy of Holies to the amazement of the people?

Indeed, the characteristics of Melchizedek argue in favor of a more spiritual interpretation of the priesthood. According to St. Paul, Melchizedek was a figure without any knowable origin, neither father nor mother. Thus, he was without race, without social status, at home anywhere and available to everyone. He served the most high God alone. This seemingly "classless" quality of the great high priest, Melchizedek, is emphasized by St. Paul as he invokes him as the role-model for the priesthood of Jesus Christ.

It is in this priesthood of Melchizedek, the king of "righteousness and peace," that all Christians are called to participate. No longer does birth or hierarchy matter, and neither do laws concerning blood sacrifice, for the spiritual sacrifice of a "*broken and contrite heart*" (Ps 51: 17), through the Holy Spirit and by the power of the saving Passion of Christ, has become the matter to be offered up, so that God Himself may enter into the heart of those who love Him.

The royal priesthood of Melchizedek passes through Christ to his people. A priesthood of peace and righteousness, it is bestowed on all those who pray to Him "*in peace*," something of which no one attentive to Orthodox worship, with its reiterated invitation "*Again and again in peace let us pray unto the Lord!*" can long remain unaware.

That reign of peace, whatever it may be with it being so vulgarly bandied about at Christmas time each year, is always an interior peace. It is the peace "*from on high*" that allows us, in the midst of the greatest cataclysm, to offer up the whole world in a "*mercy of peace*" in the one "*sacrifice of praise*" given us by Christ in the Divine Liturgy.

The essential thing is that this royal priesthood of righteousness and peace has been bestowed on all who have put on Christ in baptism. As an Orthodox Christian, one is called upon to exercise this priesthood of righteousness and peace where there is no distinction between male and female, for all are called, all are summoned.

Being of a far more universal order than the hierarchical priesthood, "*the priesthood of all believers*" was brilliantly illustrated by the quip of the late Mother Teresa of Calcutta when asked by a journalist what she thought of all those Roman Catholic nuns in America who were struggling to become priests. Mother Teresa snapped back with no hesitation whatsoever, "*There's no greater priest than Our Lady.*"

Inasmuch as St. Paul sees Jesus Christ Himself as the one who revived the priesthood of Melchizedek, the eternal dimension of such a priesthood stretches far beyond that of the high priest in Jerusalem offering animal sacrifices for specific events or on specific days for the specific sins of a specific people. The priesthood of Melchizedek is that exercised by any Orthodox believer who, while still on this planet, makes of every day granted him an occasion, through the Holy Spirit, for uniting his earthly life to God in Christ as he intercedes for the world and for all men.

It was in exercising this priesthood that female saints such as St. Nina and St. Photini went forth to preach the Gospel. Both male and female baptized Christians were given the grace to bear witness in this world both as kings and priests, according to St. John's Apocalypse (Rev 1:6), to show Him forth that others may see Him and glorify the heavenly Father.

According to Georgian tradition, even the Godbirthgiver herself was part of this effort at female evangelization. This tradition says that, when the Apostles were dividing up the world as mission field for evangelization, our all-holy and ever-virgin Lady said that Georgia would be hers. The Athonite tradition that a field of lilies still marks to this day the site of her landing on Mount Athos is in no way contradictory to this Georgian tradition that she went to announce the Good News in Georgia.

v

The challenge of being a priest is, therefore, one which every lover of Christ must face as a responsible, baptized Christian. Not only is every lover of Christ bound to pray for all men and for the whole world, as is done formally at every Divine Liturgy, but he is also called to join himself to Christ in being continually offered up to the Father, through the Holy Spirit, with Christ Himself "*on behalf of all, and for all.*" Indeed, the "*more excellent way*" of living, as the holy Apostle teaches us, is that of love, of charity for all. And he who loves automatically opens himself to suffering, even as the Lord Himself did in deigning to love us and in emptying Himself of His glory for us.

116

THE HEART OF ORTHODOX MYSTERY

To love another makes great demands on our capabilities, for one never knows what the well-being of the other may entail. Christian glory in marriage is never to be discerned just in the vibrant and elated beautiful young couple who look so radiant on their wedding day. It is equally discernable in that same couple 30 or 40 years later, when, in spite of ageing and infirmities, the spouses still cling to each other just as they promised God they would love one another in Christ regardless of what happened following their wedding day. As with all things pertaining to God, conjugal fidelity, like monastic fidelity, is beyond human logic since it is a grace, given by God.

The quantity of sacrifices demanded in any marriage is incalculable, as are also the quantity demanded in rearing children. These demands made both by marriage and by childbearing constantly require an inward, spiritual renewal of love. How vital this daily spiritual renewal is in the ongoing business of rearing children, the demands of which are often even more acute than those encountered with one's spouse. At the heart of the family unit, therefore, one must seek not just formless, mindless "happily-ever-after" love, but love that is strong enough to be incarnate before the world as what it truly is when stripped of its romantic trappings: endless, boundless sacrifice, humbly repeated again and again until one's last breath. That is the highest love.

One understands, therefore, that exercising one's sacrificial priesthood stretches far beyond the purely ecclesiastical aspects of one's life, even though it is in that holy dimension of one's life that all sacrifice, as well as all selfless love, finds both its source and its anchor. But the priesthood of being a Christian spouse or a Christian parent does demand that all of one's life in Christ be applied to both those states of spouse and parent. The same is also true for a monastic who strives to become a true monk, truly living alone with God.

While one rightly speaks of the monastic life as being the "angelic life" and, thus, a higher calling than married life since one is able to give oneself more freely to prayer, there is still only one true sanctity, and that sanctity is the sanctity of God alone, not of a state of life. The state of life, monastic or married, does not in itself sanctify the person choosing it; rather, the holiness of God alone sanctifies it. Such holiness can be found in

117

all life that is truly lived in Christ through the Holy Spirit to the glory of the Father. That alone sanctifies man and makes of him a saint.

vi

In the Holy Tradition of the Orthodox Church, it is the Holy Spirit, not a Pope or a Patriarch, who has always presided over the Church. He has ever been the *"Heavenly King and Comforter,"* indeed, the *only* Comforter that suffering Christians, through the prayers of their holy fathers and mothers, can rely upon to reveal Christ to them in the midst of tribulations.

The Church is never more truly the Bride of Christ, the mystical Spouse of her thorn-crowned and flagellated Bridegroom, than when she finds herself glorified by the marks of His Passion that she is called upon to share with Him. For then the Spirit truly rests upon her. The perennial blood of the martyrs dyes her vesture indelibly before men and angels with the royal purple of the Church's eternal and uncreated majesty, that same timeless majesty she worships in the sacred wounds of her crucified Lord and God.

Orthodoxy does not differentiate, as does the Western Church, between the "Church militant," the "Church expectant" or the "Church triumphant," since there never can be but one Church in Orthodox thinking. The purpose of that Church, moreover, is to unite both the living and the dead, along with all those yet to come, into one Mystical Body. She continually prays, *"Thine own, of thine own, we offer unto Thee, on behalf of all, and for all,"* that all may be made one in Christ and in His unique sacrifice. By this prayer, Christ does become all in all for His mystical Bride. The heart of the Orthodox lover of Christ thus beats in harmony with St. John the Theologian when he writes:

> *And the Spirit and the bride say, Come. And let him that heareth say, Come. And let him that is athirst come. And whosoever will, let him take the water of life freely.* (Rev 22:17)

118

For it is only in Him who has come, and still comes, and who is to come again, that every member of His Mystical Body finds meaning to his existence. The constant prayer of the lover of Christ to Him becomes: "*Come quickly!*" (Rev.12:20). One thereby echoes the conclusion of the Eucharistic prayer found in the *Didache*: "*Let grace come and let this world pass away!*"

Given Orthodoxy's view of the mystery of the Church as an eternal mystery that is constantly being lived by all who have put on Christ, there is, therefore, no real place in Orthodox thinking for the Western divisions of the Church of God into three parts: the Church militant being the Church on earth, the Church expectant being those who are dead but not yet glorified, and the Church triumphant being that of the saints. These categories are far too neat and rational to accord with the spiritual and cosmic reality that is the ever-dynamic life of the Holy Spirit residing in the Church of God.

In Holy Orthodoxy, all who have put on Christ are potentially in Christ, and Christ is beyond division or measurement by schedules of time. True, the Lord is yet to come to fulfill all things; yet, in a very real, concrete and tangible sense mystically, the Lord does come and does fulfill all things each time the Holy Liturgy is celebrated. For the Orthodox, it is as if one were already, in this life, moving in that uncreated time of eternity, since one has been baptized into an eternal, uncreated God. One has put on Christ, and Christ dwells in those who are His. It was undoubtedly an acute sense of this "more abundant" life given only in Christ that enabled so many martyrs to rise above the expected pains of the torments inflicted on them, since these earthly things are effective only when one is limited by the earthly state. But in Christ, the eternal Divine Logos of God, one can do all things (Phil 4:13).

Certainly, the idea of the "Church militant," so cherished in the West, has often proven nefarious in its application. It fits so admirably into Roman Catholicism's power structure, making the Church on earth a sort of police force to impose its feudal structure: the Pope is at the top of a vast global pyramid and is responsible for imposing the true Roman faith on this world for which, after all, the Lord refused to pray (Jn 17:9). To the end of serving this worldly, feudal structure, the Church militant feels justified in executing heretics and infidels, in launching crusades, or, as is the "ecumenical style" of the latest Pope, in going about asking forgiveness of the living for those long since dead while, at the same time, surreptitiously strengthening the political power base of the Roman Church. The mind-set whereby the Papacy was imposed on the Western Church as a human organism with divine pretensions, even to the blasphemous extent of proclaiming that whosoever was elected to the Papacy was, come what may, "Christ's Vicar on earth," has been raised by Roman Catholicism to a matter of faith equal in importance to the Holy Trinity. This, however, is a highly different mind-set from that of Orthodox Christians.

This is why only an Orthodox Christian can seize the vast, cosmic horror implied in the sorrowing observation of the late blessed Serbian Elder, Father Justin Popovich, who equated the rise of the Papacy to the Fall of the Holy Roman Church of God. That holy elder of blessed memory observed that there have been three great Falls in creation: that of Lucifer, that of Adam, and that of the Church of Rome in giving rise to the subtle idolatry inevitably inherent in the Papacy.

As for the Orthodox mind-set, it ever remains open to the necessity of man's working *with* God in determining the Church's fate on earth through martyrdom, as did the early Christians. Indeed, in Orthodox history, martyrdom has never been too far removed from the believers' experience. The thought that I and my fellow believers may be called upon to save the Orthodox faith by suffering for it engenders in the individual believer a highly personal sense of responsibility for the survival of the Church of God on earth. This basis of operation is, thus, very far removed from that confident Western believer who looks to a great worldly power-structure such as the Vatican-led Roman Catholic Church to guarantee the survival of the faith, whether or not he actually participates.

On the surface, of course, the Roman Catholic point of view seems far safer, less risky, and more reassuring than trying to make one's own the admonition of St. Seraphim: "*Save yourself and you'll save a thousand.*" Yet, within the mystery of the Church, the true glorification of the Church can come only from being members of the Body of Christ, which is the Church, as well as from being glorified with and in Christ. And since the uncreated glorification of Mount Tabor is rooted in the passion and death of His "*coming decease,*" the Orthodox Christian, in anticipating martyrdom as a quite natural part of Christian life, does not, as it were,

120

hesitate to reach out towards that uncreated glory of Mount Tabor in a way that the more secure Western believer usually sees no real need to risk doing.

In the final analysis, of course, within the mystery of the Church, martyrdom can never be avoided by any man. It is truly inevitable, since each man's death is assigned to him as his final witness - or, in Greek, *martyrdom* - by which his life is crowned. Blessed is the man whose death serves to glorify God!

The Roman Catholic has the luxury of basking confidently in the power-structure of the "Holy Mother Church," which he trusts will always save not only him, but also the Church in the world. Vatican-inspired, pro-papal propaganda does nothing but reinforce this false and erroneously placed confidence that the Church of God is, indeed, actually something *other* than its members, that it is, in fact, something quite *other* than oneself and in no way directly related to one's own personal struggles to save one's soul. In contrast, how peculiarly Orthodox sounds St. Seraphim's saying, *"Save your own soul and you'll save a thousand!"* The directness implied by the workings of the Holy Spirit between the believer and the cosmos is quietly present in St. Seraphim's thought, as is also the blessed total absence of bureaucratic salvation that is achieved by committees and hierarchical decisions or an exalted, infallible "Vicar of Christ on earth" presiding over the salvation of the human race.

That the Church is, indeed, rooted in the continued, personal confession that Jesus Christ is God can only imply that every believer, exercising the priesthood of righteousness and peace belonging to Melchizedek and into which he was baptized in putting on Christ, must bear as much responsibility for living out the truth of that faith as any priest, bishop, archbishop, pope or patriarch. There must, therefore, be a personal response in every believer to the Holy Spirit's summons to glory. That response must spontaneously, and from love, spring from the believer's heart rather than his head, that he himself may truly be a priest of righteousness and peace.

The challenge of answering the summons to accept this vocation is indeed the challenge constantly confronting every believer within the mystery of the Church. It is the challenge offered all those called to the "order of Melchizedek," a priesthood based not on birth or worldly status, but on having truly "put on Christ" in baptism and on freely sharing in His self-offering for the cosmos, according to the grace given each of us through the mercy of God, by the intercessions of the saints.

CHAPTER IX

The Heart of "The Fellowship of His Sufferings"

Orthodoxy's most prevalent and identifiable image is not the ever-present crucifix, so intimately associated with Roman Catholicism, but rather the icon of the Virgin Godbirthgiver holding her divine Son. Does Orthodoxy, then, shy away from the cross or from the mystery of its suffering?

The cross is, in fact, the subject of particular honor in Orthodoxy. The solemn celebration of the feast of the Exaltation of the Holy Cross on September 14, besides being accompanied by a strict fast, is one of the 12 Great Feasts in the Orthodox liturgical year. In addition, the third Sunday of Great Lent is also centered on the veneration of the Cross, which is presented to the faithful on that Sunday in the middle of Lent surrounded with flowers. This is intended as a sign of encouragement to the fasting faithful as they continue their yearly struggle towards Pascha. The hymn sung repeatedly during the procession on that day as the kneeling faithful bow prostrate before the flower-bedecked cross as it passes -- *"Lord thy Cross do we venerate, and thy holy Resurrection do we glorify!"* -- typifies the very healthy liturgical balance Orthodoxy insists upon in regard to the cross: never is it to be separated from the Resurrection.

It can, moreover, never be recalled too often that the Orthodox Church sings the long and glorious text of the Canon of the Harrowing of Hell not only on Good Friday night at the service of Lamentations over the tomb of the dead Christ, but also on Holy Saturday night. The singing of the Canon is, in fact, terminated just prior to the distribution of the holy light of Pascha to the people for the outdoor procession, with its announcement of the Resurrection and the great outbursts of rejoicing that immediately follow.

It is, therefore, not surprising that, within the mystery of the Church, the joy of the Christian is always that of the Lord's final triumph over suffering and death. He, the Lord of Glory, even as He Himself prayed, did not ascend to his place on the Father's right hand without first having been glorified through His suffering and death on the cross. His glorification by suffering and death was, as we have repeatedly observed, the subject on which He discoursed with Moses and Elijah at His wondrous Transfiguration on Mt. Tabor. Moreover, on the night when He was betrayed, He was indeed referring to His suffering and death on the cross that was to take place the next day as He prayed to be glorified by the Father, that men might see the glory He shared with the Father before the world began (Jn 17:5).

If, within the mystery of the Church, we aspire to grasp what is essential to the holy Apostles' teaching on suffering in general, as well as on the sufferings of Christ Himself, we are obliged to recognize that, repeatedly and with some insistence, Christ's glorification is intimately and inextricably fused with His suffering. *"Slain from the foundation of the world"* (Rev 13:8), He, the mystic Lamb of God, Jesus Christ, the eternal Logos and only-begotten Son of the Father, grasped in His humanity as well as in His divinity, along with the great Jewish patriarchs Moses and Elijah, the essential, yet paradoxical, nature of His sacrifice on Calvary. Therein the Lord of Glory Himself was to suffer and die in extreme humility: stripped naked, flagellated, spat upon, buffeted and mocked by His creatures.

The Lord's sacrifice on Calvary was not "just another sacrifice," but the one supreme recapitulation and cosmic sacrifice of the Word and only-begotten Son of God Who, as one of the Godhead, incarnate in the flesh, was offering Himself to the Father that His human suffering and death might perfectly fulfill that complete and perfect humanity He had assumed from the most holy Theotokos. Thus, man might come to understand that *"the Lamb slain from the foundation of the world"* (Rev 13:8) was not something forever removed from human experience and in the realm of the Godhead alone, but, through the Incarnation of Jesus Christ, something that has become relevant to all lovers of Christ.

ii

In evoking the vision of the Lamb slain from the foundation of the world in the last book of the New Testament, St. John the Theologian, the beloved disciple, there actually recapitulates the announcement that he alone among the four Evangelists attributes to St. John the Baptist at the moment that Jesus Christ was coming to be baptized prior to beginning his brief ministry. The Forerunner of Christ had pointed to Him and proclaimed, "*Behold the Lamb of God which teeth away the sin of the world*" (Jn 1:29), thus revealing to the human race that the cosmic mystery of the eventual sacrifice on Calvary was, indeed, situated at the very heart of His Incarnation. Understanding who Jesus Christ is, therefore, is a matter of major importance for all who love Christ and have put Him on in Baptism. In Him, and in His Incarnation, is to be discovered the eternal truth regarding the mystery of creation itself. Indeed, understanding Him as the one great, eternal and universal Victim, slain from the foundation of the world, becomes a means whereby man is led ineluctably by the Holy Spirit into the eternal mysteries of God.

No less than St. Paul throughout his writings, St. Peter, in his First Epistle, insists upon the very close ties Christians share with Jesus Christ through their sufferings. St. Peter regards Christians in their struggles as "*good stewards of the manifold grace of God*" (I Pet 4:10). It is for this reason that he admonishes them, "*Think it not strange concerning the fiery trial which is to try you, as though some strange thing had happened unto you*" (I Pet 4: 12), then concludes with this admonition:

> *Rejoice inasmuch as ye are partakers of Christ's sufferings: that when his glory shall be revealed, ye may be glad also with exceeding joy.* (I Pet 4:13)

Genuine Christian joy is, therefore, to be discovered in sharing in the sufferings of Christ. Through this fellowship, one is called upon to glorify God through one's personal sufferings, just as Jesus Christ was called upon to glorify God in a like manner. This is not to say, of course, that Christians are against joy in any way. St. Paul urges his converts to "*rejoice in the Lord*" (Phil 13:1). Yet, the Lord Himself reminds us that the joy that He gives us is a joy that can never be taken away by any man, unlike the frenzied, fevered joy given by the world and in evidence at sporting events.

Towards the end of his Epistle to the Philippians, St. Paul, beginning his conclusion with the phrase, "*Finally, my brethren, rejoice in the Lord"* (Phil 4:4), proceeds not only to proclaim his impeccably high qualifications for being a Jew of the best pedigree, but resumes his arguments by declaring, *"But what things were gain to me, those I counted loss for Christ"* (Phil 3:7). He clearly shows that his rejoicing in the Lord is far, indeed, from normal rejoicing in the world.

This statement, in turn, leads into the magnificent statement of that Christocentric life that had become the life of St. Paul, a life so centered on Christ and, through the Holy Spirit, so filled with Christ that, to this day, the Spirit-filled energy it continues to radiate still sustains and encourages Christians throughout the world. Indeed, his life has inspired and sustained millions of the faithful since the dawning of the Christian faith with passages such as this one to the Philippians, from which the title of our chapter is drawn.

> *Yea doubtless, and I count all things but loss for the excellency of the knowledge of Christ Jesus my Lord: for whom I have suffered the loss of all things, and do count them but dung, that I may win Christ. And be found in Him, not having mine own righteousness, which is of the law, but that which is through the faith of Christ, the righteousness which is of God by faith: that I may know him, and the power of his resurrection, and the fellowship of his sufferings, being made conformable unto his death* (Phil 3:8-10).

The lover of Christ who seeks Christ in all His fullness in Orthodoxy and becomes familiar with the sufferings in the lives of the saints as presented in the *Synaxarion*[8] will inevitably find reason to pause before the striking phrase, *"fellowship of his sufferings."* Is this truly an accurate image of what St. Paul believed to be the vocation of a Christian? Is consenting to participate in the *"fellowship of his sufferings"* required of us?

Certainly, if we are to participate in the God-inspired pattern set for us by St. Paul himself, our continued, ongoing assent to participate in the

---

[8] See Note 1, p. 7.

"*fellowship of His sufferings*" becomes the way by which we prove ourselves as lovers of Christ. St. Paul's own sorrowing and persecuted, yet glorious miracle-working ministry has repeatedly shown us what it means to become a glorious and sanctified member of "*the fellowship of His sufferings*."

iii

Any thinking man, be he Christian or non-Christian, cannot but discover that suffering is always a basic element of life. Some sort of suffering almost always seems demanded of everyone in one form or another, be it the hidden mental and emotional sufferings and stress of everyday life, or great and extraordinary physical or mental sufferings, or handicaps given to some to bear until their last breath. Whether it be the newborn making its crying way into the world or the dying, aged soul struggling to leave the world and impotent to take anything with him, life is always a struggle. The only difference between the Christian and the non-Christian is that the lover of Christ has the great grace of knowing that he is able to suffer within the mystery of the Church and, therefore, in union with Christ's sufferings. Every Christian is, indeed, encompassed by that great "*cloud of witnesses*" (Heb 12:1) who have gone before him and whose sufferings long before his own have also been united to the sufferings of Christ.

Suffering is, indeed, the one truly basic human tie binding all men to one another as brothers. For Christians, suffering provides the one common bond forever exalted and raised to the right hand of the Father through the glorified wounds of the risen Christ. Thus, suffering not only challenges the basic doctrine of American Civil Religion, that is, "*the pursuit of happiness*," but, as we have seen, rises in blatant opposition to it, showing it to be based on a very shallow, thoughtless evaluation both of life and of life's potential and purpose.

In Beethoven's Ninth Symphony, the composer, attuned to the 19th century fashion of trying to deliver some sort of universal message for all mankind, impressively set the 18th century text of Friedrich Schiller's "Ode to Joy" to music for choir and orchestra. The Schiller text is incorporated into the last, glorious movement of the composer's last symphony, as if it were his final message to the world, holding up joy as the one true universal value capable of binding all men together as brothers.

Both Schiller and Beethoven seem to have forgotten, however, that human joy is far less a universal given than is human sorrow. Men can universally discover their true brotherhood only through the thorough-going fellowship of their sufferings, not through the more selective fellowship of their joys. All mothers who have lost a child are sisters forever in a sense that all men who are warriors can never be brothers, since the joyous victory of one signals the defeat of another.

The idea of *"the fellowship of his sufferings,"* quite unlike the *"inalienable right to the pursuit of happiness"* or Schiller's "Ode to Joy," is concerned only with the *"Great Mercy"* of the eternal truth that has been given the world through the coming of our Lord, God and Saviour Jesus Christ. For He did not come just to save us from our sins through his sacrifice, though this is true. Nor did He come just to reveal the Holy Trinity to mankind, which is also true. Moving beyond both of these very valid reasons for the Incarnation, one discovers as one lives out one's life that there is yet another, equally universal reason that was obviously very close to the heart of St. Paul.

This reason is that of His showing us, through His coming to us in the Incarnation, that through our sufferings, and through joining our sufferings to His own, our very ordinary lives can be intimately related to His life, the life of Him who proclaimed that He was Himself *"the way, the truth, and the life"* (Jn 14:6). For He is the uncreated divine Logos, by Whom all things were made.

The relationship between God and man suddenly takes on seemingly endless and infinite dimensions when a Christian learns to offer up his own sufferings to Christ that they might be incorporated into Christ's sufferings. In what sharp contrast does a lifetime of offering up one's sufferings stand when set against a whole lifetime devoted to nursing grudges against God's goodness.

Christians are, therefore, given the grace, through the Holy Spirit, to be able to accept, in the Name of Jesus Christ, the sufferings allotted them and even to embrace them for His sake, offering them up in union with His own sufferings. Has He not taught us that, in Him, all our sufferings are neither vain, nor absurd, nor without relevance to our own salvation? His coming has empowered man to make use of all the unpleasant experiences of life, even the most absurd and inexplicable ones. Because of Christ, and because of Christ's sufferings, man's own sufferings are no longer insignificant. Indeed, because of Christ, man himself is no longer insignificant: he has been bought by the blood of incarnate God Himself.

This realization can prove potentially healing for those who feel they are totally trapped in sufferings rooted in events that are hard to forgive, whether they were abandoned, mistreated, persecuted or abused as a child, for example, or impaired for life through an accident of birth or circumstances. In Christ, however, *all* is reconciled, *nothing* is held back. Indeed, Orthodox Christians are reminded annually, each time they sing the Pascal verses throughout the 40 days of Paschaltide, that all has been reconciled in the Resurrection of Christ:

> *It is the Day of Resurrection!*
> *Let us be illumined by the Feast!*
> *Let us embrace each other!*
> *Let us call 'Brothers' even those that hate us,*
> *And forgive all by the Resurrection!*

The lover of Christ, therefore, accepts all his sufferings not only *for* Christ, but also *by* Christ and *in* Christ, thereby uniting them *to* Christ and to His sufferings. Through the risen Christ alone do man's sufferings have the potential of becoming redemptive energies not only for himself, but for the entire world. Through them, the lover of Christ, hidden in Christ, thus becomes an active participant in the mystery of the Church's ongoing redemptive action in the world. At the proclamation, "*Thine own, of thine own, we offer unto thee, in behalf of all, and for all,*" the Orthodox lover of Christ learns to offer up his sufferings in union with those of Christ at each Divine Liturgy.

So it is that in God's great mercy, and through the Holy Spirit, our Lord and God, Jesus Christ Himself comes to touch the psychic wounds of all who love Him. The lover of Christ even discovers that through such intimate union with Christ true healing is to be found. Man is no longer afraid of his deepest wounds, nor is he any longer alone with them. There, where those wounds are found, deep within his interior life, the Lord Himself awaits, saying as He once said to the fearful disciples who saw Him walking on the sea and moving towards their boat in the middle of the night, *"It is I: be not afraid"* (Mat 14:27).

As one of the holy fathers wisely observed, *"The thought of God saves us."*

iv

Surely, if we can rejoice as Christians, it is never, as St. Paul insists, because we rejoice in our own righteousness. The only righteousness we have is *"that which is through the faith of Christ, the righteousness which is of God by faith"* (Phil 3:9), as the holy Apostle writes. Because we do not have our own righteousness, we are totally dependent on Him for any meaning at all to be given our existence. Through the Divine Liturgy, we therefore learn to participate, once weekly at least, in offering ourselves with Him for the salvation of the world.

On the surface, this may seem a rather warped, unbalanced and extremely gloomy view of what the Christian faith is all about. We may even be tempted to dismiss the *"fellowship of his sufferings"* as something not of our times, thinking as we do that 21st century man is totally different from man of the time of the St. Paul. One might even argue, "The *'fellowship of his sufferings'* obviously existed in St. Paul's mind, but must we really dwell on it? Granted, the martyrs did die brave and laudatory deaths, but what does that really have to do with us today in the 21st century in North America? That was a long time ago and we have evolved a lot since then."

Anyone who is at all sensitive to what is going on spiritually around him, however, cannot but reach the conclusion that suffering has by no means changed. It is the one unchanging law of life, constituting life's most persistent fabric and, indeed, the most basic fact of living. The great French Christian poet Charles Baudelaire once observed that the daily newspaper, read with one's breakfast coffee in the morning, is actually a *"fabric of horrors,"* since it is filled with account after account of the sufferings of mankind. The type of suffering reported each day is a matter of total indifference both for the journalists who write and for the readers who read what they write. The newsworthy fact is rooted in one simple truth: suffering exists and continues to take on new and surprising forms. Newspaper headlines may spring as easily from the injustices suffered by the innocent as from the administration of human justice. An execution, for example, is always newsworthy, regardless of how lowly the victim, how obscure the crime or how far removed the place where it took place.

V

The Latin language, in using the same word for "suffering" that is used for "passion," has given us, as part of our Western Christian heritage, the ability to speak quite comfortably of the Lord's Passion and Death while understanding with no difficulty that we actually mean His *sufferings* and death. Yet, in general use, *"passion"*[9] normally describes a state prompted more by amorous desire than by the desire to suffer. Nonetheless, a stark truth remains, one which most will instinctively want to reject: *"to love is to suffer."*

However, when one thinks of love beyond that of amorous desire, that of a parent for a child, for example, it is still true that *"to love is to suffer."* What Christian parent could deny this truth? And even regarding amorous desires, what lover has not suffered and does not continue to suffer, as long as he loves, whether from fear of loss of the beloved or of some ill befalling the beloved?

While these may seem very humble images to associate with the sufferings of Christ, they are fairly universal images and are familiar to

---

[9] "Passion" or "the passions" are terms used, of course, by the Holy Fathers to explain the demonic tools behind much of man's comportment in life, be it the passion for wealth, success, glory or any other preoccupation that is not God Himself. Whence the exaltation of the state of "passionlessness," wherein man has freed himself from passions. The frequent translation of this term by "dispassion" does not really serve spiritual clarity, since being dispassionate about something implies a certain indifference, which is far from being the case.

131

most readers. And man's most intimate sufferings, within the divine economy, and by God's great mercy, are not at all to be excluded from association with Christ's sufferings. Indeed, one comes to understand that the sufferings of Christ, within the mystery of the Church, are not intended at all to be distant or far-removed from our most intimate, humble and ordinary human experience. One may say, of course, that, in the end, it is not the actual suffering that makes a spiritual difference; rather, it is what we make of the suffering endured that is important. Whatever the case, it is only through man's suffering that the power, the love and the might of Christ can be invited into man's soul to heal the unhealable.

A murderer, for example, can never undo his victim's death any more than a mother can ever undo the abortion of her unborn child. Enlightened by the Holy Spirit, one finds the memory of such actions and the guilt associated with them to be unbearable. The "natural" reaction is to try and get over it, to push it all aside, to try to forget it all, to bury it, to sweep it under the carpet, as it were. But these efforts are certainly far from being either satisfactory or universally successful. Through the Holy Spirit, one is actually led to accept the enlightened fact that these memories can, in fact, never be pushed aside. Even though the sin has been assumed by Christ Himself, the Holy Spirit, the Spirit of Truth, still causes man to pray, to reach out, as it were, and to lay hold of Christ's saving and healing power to "*make all things new*" (Rev 21:5). Otherwise, how can man not prove that he is utterly helpless in trying to deal with these great, mind-boggling mysteries of good and evil in human existence? Only a man-loving God could come close enough to man to share in such intimate sorrows of a contrite heart. Do we not have the Psalmist's hope, "*A broken and a contrite heart, O God, wilt thou not despise*" (Ps 51: 17)?

The tide of man's sin covered by the blood of Christ at the time of the crucifixion stretched universally even to the depths of Hades, to which He descended to bring forth Adam and Eve and all their descendants and place them in His kingdom and under the reign of the Holy Trinity. He shed His blood that He might cover all sin, taking it upon Himself, so that the guilty, in Him, might finally find that true peace which the world can never give. He, through his *kenosis,* so emptied Himself of His uncreated glory that, in His great mercy, He stooped low enough to assume all human sin, identifying Himself with every sinner and with every sin. *"Glory to thy condescension, O Lord! Glory to Thee!"*

It is important, therefore, for the lover of Christ, as for St. Mary of Egypt, to recognize that it is, in fact, through the shame, regret, and sense of the abyss of one's own sinfulness that the Lord, through the Holy Spirit, reveals His greatness, showing us that He Himself must truly become our righteousness, for man, of himself, has no righteousness to offer Him. Indeed, it is only when man discovers that he has only Christ as his righteousness that he can begin to desire to be seen in Him alone, as it were a feeble, tarnished and so imperfect reflection of His sacred face. As the repentant St. Mary of Egypt might have prayed, so too might he pray with tears: *"It is enough indeed, O Lord, that Thou art in truth my Lord and my God, for thou hast covered my sin and made all things new. Beside this great gift I desire no other!"*

vi

It is, indeed, through the *"fellowship of his sufferings"* that all the saints and confessors and martyrs of the Orthodox Church are united not only *in* Him and *to* Him, but also, through the Holy Spirit, to one another and to all those who have suffered for Him in the past. They are also, through the mystery of the Church, united to those who, by God's grace, are yet destined to bear witness to Him in the future through their sufferings, for the Lord wills that His glory continue to be manifest throughout His creation, for the world is indeed vast and God's ineffable creation is immense. Yet, beyond and above it all, pouring forth from the risen Christ, is the great mercy of God, sustaining all things through the Holy Spirit.

The miracle of the mystery of the Church, therefore, allows the new Orthodox convert in the 21st century to experience, through the *"fellowship of his sufferings,"* a profound union with the whole of those millions who have borne witness to God in Jesus Christ. The mystery of the Church also unites the lover of Christ to *"every righteous soul made perfect who since the beginning of time has glorified God,"* that is, those righteous witnesses coming before Jesus Christ.

This is because our sharing in the sufferings of Christ not only profoundly identifies us with Him, but also raises us to the status of children of God, as the holy Apostle states in the Epistle to the Romans:

The Spirit itself beareth witness with our spirit, that we are the children of God: and if children, then heirs: heirs of God and joint-heirs with Christ; if so be that we suffer with him, that we may be also glorified together (Rom 8:16-17).

Indeed, if one thinks of the company of the saints, martyrs and confessors who stand before the throne of God and, with the angels, sing never ending praises to God, one might well ask what would really be the most glorious mark of fidelity that a lover of Christ might bear before the face of God. Just as at the First Ecumenical Council in Nicea in 325, where the bodies of many of the 318 bishops present were mutilated from the loss of eyes or noses or from calcified limbs resulting from fiery tortures, all simply because they maintained that Jesus Christ was God, so do martyrs' scars gained from suffering for Christ still remain the proud boast of the Orthodox Church as of every Christ-loving soul. Indeed, such witnesses truly bear in their bodies the *"marks of the Lord Jesus"* (Gal 6:17), as the Holy Apostle Paul said of himself.

This same Holy Apostle, in speaking in his Epistle to the Colossians of *"making up what is lacking in the sufferings of Christ"* (Col 1:24), was obviously aware of the open-ended, ongoing nature of the Incarnation of Jesus Christ, that is, that it can never become something that can be neatly wrapped up, set up on a shelf once and for all, then consulted only when needed, as one might a reference book or an oracle. Indeed, the Incarnation, since the day of the Ascension, has ever offered man an invitation to put on Christ in Baptism and share in *"the fellowship of his sufferings."* For, within the mystery of the Church, the sufferings of Christ, and participation in them by all those who love Him, have their own dynamism and life within the Holy Spirit. In the divine life of that dynamism, both God and man are involved, joined together in divine synergy for the salvation of the cosmos. *"He that gathereth not with me scattereth abroad"* (Mat 12:30), the Lord Himself has said.

The fellowship of His sufferings is, therefore, the holy means given the human race to be able to work together with Him through the Holy Spirit. So too, let us recall, was it necessary for the most holy Godbirthgiver to work *with* the Holy Spirit to bring Him forth from her flesh in the first place. For in Orthodox teaching, we should never forget, the Godbirthgiver is seen as an *active* rather than a *passive* agent in the Incarnation of Jesus Christ. In the Greek text of the Nicene Creed, He was incarnate *"by the Holy Spirit AND the Virgin Mary,"* rather than the more passive *"OF the Virgin Mary,"* taught in the Latin text.

This principle of God and man working together, called "synergy" in Orthodox parlance, is indeed basic to all Orthodox understanding of what the Christian life is all about. So it is that Orthodoxy's insistence on the necessity for such synergetic cooperation with the Holy Spirit on the part of all believers merely upholds all the Holy Apostle teaches us about suffering with Christ in the *"fellowship of his sufferings."* There is really no place in the Christian scheme of things for a passive, indifferent adherence to Jesus Christ, that is, the adherence of the so-called "normal" Christian. The Roman Empire was correct in grasping that Christians were by no means, or in any way, "normal" people. They were profoundly countercultural because of the great intimacy they repeatedly claimed with the Uncreated God, and they remain so to this day to the extent that they are truly Christian.

An unending, lifelong struggle to bear witness to an intimate identity with Christ is certainly implied by "putting Him on" in baptism. Through the indwelling of the Holy Spirit, one's life can, indeed, become more and more integrated as it is increasingly touched by this identity and even transformed by it. Thus only does one begin to understand that *"the fellowship of his sufferings"* is not something apart from the everyday, minute-by-minute annoyances that are those of any thinking person. All that one suffers, one starts to grasp, is only a tiny part of the whole fabric of human suffering, which is, indeed, the common lot of the children of fallen Adam.

The Buddhists have as a basic principle that to live is to suffer. Not being contaminated by the illusion of an "inalienable right to the pursuit of happiness" offered by the thought of the 18th century Enlightenment, the Buddhists perhaps have less difficulty in setting their faces towards what for them is another sort of Enlightenment, offered them not by Christ, but by rising above the world to the utter nothingness of Nirvana. Whatever it may be with their Nirvana, at least they are keenly aware, unlike most North Americans, Christian or not, that suffering is within the daily order of fallen creation itself.

Christians, however, have the advantage of knowing not only that they are not suffering alone, but that through Christ and His sufferings an eternal dimension, rooted in the mystery of creation itself, has been bestowed on all suffering. That vast backdrop of suffering that automatically comes into focus through the Buddhist principle that "to live is to suffer" is, in Christianity, suddenly empowered to take on a life of its own, as well as a profound meaning. The whole fabric of life, though full of suffering, has, through the Incarnation of Jesus Christ, been given meaning -- eternal meaning -- in Him. In Him, and by the Holy Spirit, every thread composing the incomprehensible, indescribable fabric of our sorrowing life can be transfigured into a luminous grace given by the Holy Spirit so that, in the end, we too can say, as Charles Baudelaire wrote at the end of his too-brief life, "*All my humiliations have been graces.*"

vii

In honoring the sufferings of the dying destitute as the sufferings of Christ Himself, Mother Teresa of Calcutta and her sisters were merely honoring Him for whom they lived and to Whom they had consecrated their entire lives until their last breath. For it was, they believed, He who was lying there, in their midst, hidden from the non-believers under the form of some stinking, rat-gnawed helpless dying destitute, alone and in the dark.

Learning to recognize Him in their midst in the streets of Calcutta, therefore, allowed Mother Teresa and her sisters to make visible the glory of God working through them throughout the world. Mother Teresa, in her holiness, said she was grateful for the Nobel Peace Prize which constituted a public, worldwide recognition that God is at work in the world.

So too, if we are to become members of the "*fellowship of his sufferings,*" are all lovers of Christ called to perceive Him in the midst of our humble, daily struggles. The remarkable thing, and the ever-renewed miracle, is that to those holy ones of God who do willingly embrace this vocation out of love for God, the courage needed to become a partaker of the *"fellowship of his sufferings"* seems always to be given by the Holy Spirit. Where is the saint, where is the righteous, Christ-loving soul who has not embraced the *"fellowship of his sufferings"*?

"For I reckon that the sufferings of this present time are not worthy to be compared with the glory which shall be revealed to us" (Rom 8:18), St. Paul observes, and the martyrs witnessed time and again to the fact that the glory of the Lord far surpasses any horrors that man could do to them. In case after case, they voiced their conviction that their sufferings were borne out of love for Christ alone, and that they were as nothing compared with the eternity of glory that would be the martyr's lot. Indeed, that glory is none other than the Lord Himself, the King of Glory.

As we have seen, the most immediate consolation the martyrs seemed to cling to was the certainty that, through their sufferings, they were suffering intimately with Christ. As St. Felicity told her jailer, *"in that hour He will be suffering in me, for what I shall be suffering then will be for Him."* St. Paul further maintains in his Epistle to the Romans, as we have seen, that such suffering members of the Mystical Body of Christ are not only the children of God, but also the heirs of God and even *"joint-heirs with Christ; if so be that we suffer with him, that we may be also glorified together"* (Rom 8:17).

Thus, within the mystery of the Church, by suffering not only *with* Christ, but also *in* Christ and *through* Christ, one is allowed to participate in the eternal heartbeat of the Mystical Body of Christ, which is the Church. One's own suffering becomes a part of that heartbeat of the Mystical Body of Christ and provides a means of the most intimate union possible with Jesus Christ Himself. One has truly become a member of that *"fellowship of his sufferings,"* which, within the mystery of the Church, and until the coming of the Lord, will continue to make up that Body of Christ against which the gates of hell shall not prevail. For the Church of Jesus Christ, His own Mystical Body on earth, is built not on a man, but on the rock of St. Peter's confession: *"Thou art the Christ, the Son of the living God"* (Mat 16:16). The sufferings of the members of this enduring mystical Body of Christ continue to clothe her in a vesture radiant with His

Uncreated Light. In Him, the ongoing suffering of the members of His Mystical Body is given life by Him who is Life, and that Life is, indeed, the Light of men (Jn 1:4).

Such suffering, thus, no longer serves as an example of the cruelty and absurdity resulting from Adam's fall, but rather serves the Godhead alone, that Godhead in which Jesus Christ is Lord and God. *"One is holy! One is Lord! Jesus Christ to the glory of God the Father!"* Orthodox Christians sing in response to the priest's proclamation, *"Holy things are for the holy!"* as he elevates the just-sacrificed, consecrated Bread and Wine of the sacred mysteries of Christ's Body and Blood. Indeed, the fellowship of His sufferings is composed of those who are not content just to have "put Him on" in baptism, but who thereafter struggle to become holy.

Such souls become, as it were, living relics as well as living epistles. They shine before men and angels, proclaiming Jesus Christ to be God and Lord, as well as the source and the end, the final resolution of all man's striving, the Alpha and Omega of creation itself. In the fellowship of His sufferings, they are, by the grace of the Holy Spirit, allowed to sense what it is to partake of His divinity, as well as of His humanity, for He, in his *kenosis* of emptying out of Himself, has deigned to allow men to become *"partakers of the divine nature"* (2 Peter 1:4), as the holy Apostle Peter has written.

Such is the basic challenge presented every lover of Christ.

CHAPTER X

The Heart of "The Mystery Which hath been Hid from Ages"

St. Paul wrote to the Colossians that he was a minister of "*the mystery which hath been hid from ages*" (Col 1: 26), a striking expression, faithfully echoed in a liturgical text of the Orthodox Church:

> *The mystery which was hidden from everlasting,*
> *And unknown of the angels, O Theotokos,*
> *was revealed through thee to those who dwelt upon earth [...]*
> (Vesperal Theotokion for Tone 4)

This association of St. Paul's "*mystery which hath been hid from ages*" with the most holy Godbirthgiver will probably, at first encounter, startle many Protestants. Are we not dealing with the cosmos as a whole? What could the Virgin Mother of Jesus Christ possibly have to do with all that?

In fact, however, it is only through grasping what, through her, was, for the first time, offered the race of men that we can really begin to catch a glimpse of what the Orthodox like to call the great "philanthropy" of God. Through her, He, out of His love for men, was enabled actually to empty Himself of His uncreated glory in order to descend to men in the form of Jesus Christ. Furthermore, since the mysteries of God usually seem so totally removed from the realm of our human experience, by means of her who gave Him birth, those mysteries became visible and could be seen interacting with her in her human state of motherhood. The most holy Godbirthgiver, after all, neither was a goddess, nor was she divine, but one of our own human race.

It is, thus, with grateful, marveling wonder that the Orthodox sing at the end of the *Little Supplicatory Canon* (*Parakleisis*) to the Theotokos, "*O inexplicable wonder, that Thou didst milk-feed the Master!*" This humble, so human image expresses Orthodoxy's deep awe, humility and love before Almighty God who thus deigned to empty Himself of His glory in order to enter into the world as one of us. This final hymn of the *Parakleisis* is, moreover, often accompanied by the marveling tears of the faithful, overcome by the "*inexplicable wonder*" that Almighty God once suckled a woman's breast.

St. Paul, of course, immediately draws us out of ourselves in focusing on that "*mystery which hath been hid from ages*" (Col 1:26). He suggests for us the height, the breadth and the depth of the cosmic implications of God's coming into the world in the Person of our Lord, God and Saviour, Jesus Christ.

The quite singular and truly unique unconfused union of human nature with the divine Logos of God in Jesus Christ, moreover, actually did take place during the reign of Augustus Caesar and during St. Paul's own lifetime. It, indeed, occurred at a precise, given moment in history. The most holy Theotokos gave her assent to the Archangel Gabriel's announcement by what T. S. Eliot terms her "*barely prayable prayer*" of the Annunciation, that is, her answer to the Archangel: "*Behold the handmaid of the Lord, be it unto me according to thy word*" (Lk 1:38). Thereby she was, indeed, to become not only the bearer of Him who is in truth that "*Holy One Who (...) shall be called Son of God*" (Lk 2:35), but was also to prove herself "*full of grace*" as the Mother of our God. In the mystery of the Church, she was also to become a sort of prototype for every Christian soul. All lovers of Christ are, to this day, still called, like her, to make room within themselves for the Son of God that the compassionate Christ may be shown forth from them to the world as He continues to be shown forth from her.

The most holy Theotokos, having brought Him forth, thereafter has never ceased to point to Him, rather than to herself. She is, indeed, a living sign for the universe not only that God exists, but that He was incarnate of her. One, therefore, cannot denigrate her without denigrating the Incarnation itself, since her whole *raison d'être* within the mystery of the Church is that of pointing towards the Incarnation of Almighty God in her divine Son, Jesus Christ.

St. Paul never backed away either from these quite substantial and totally comprehensive claims made by Christianity in regard to the Incarnation of God in Jesus Christ, nor from the really essential, central claim of Christianity to which the holy Apostle returns again and again.

THE HEART OF ORTHODOX MYSTERY

That is the idea that Christ intimately abides in those who love Him. Is this not already implied in the holy Apostle's text sung at Orthodox baptisms: *"As many of you as were baptized into Christ have put on Christ! Alleluia!"*

ii

One is, thus, faced not just with a single impossibility, but with two. First, the impossibility of the Incarnation having taken place in the first place, unless, indeed, the order of nature were overthrown; and second, the impossibility of Christ's still actually being able to be "in us," something equally impossible without the order of nature being overthrown. Even to envisage -- and much more to believe -- this double impossibility, one must, of course, be totally submitted to the movement of the Holy Spirit. It is the Holy Spirit who teaches the lover of Christ, in a hidden, sacred manner, all those things pertaining to the mysteries of God and Jesus Christ that normally surpass human understanding.

Orthodox Christianity does not back away from such "impossibilities" lying at the very basis of Christianity. Orthodoxy understands that if one is thinking in only human terms, one sees nothing but "impossibilities." Nor does Orthodoxy apologize for such complexities and seeming impossibilities. It is for this reason that one is reminded in Orthodox liturgical texts that *"when God so wills, the order of nature is overcome."*

Indeed, is the whole of the Christian faith not, in fact, posited on the "impossibility" that Jesus Christ is the eternally-begotten Logos of Almighty God existing from the beginning as the Second Person of the Holy Trinity? At the same time, does holy Orthodoxy ever fail to proclaim that this eternally begotten Logos of the Father was born from the flesh of the Virgin Mary and made man during the reign of Augustus Caesar? During the reign of Tiberius Caesar was He not crucified, after which He died and was buried before rising from the tomb on the third day?

This so blatant defiance of human reasoning and human ability to comprehend, however, is in no way more "impossible" than the fusion of human nature with the Godhead of Jesus Christ, which is the whole basis for the continuation of Christianity over the past 2,000 years. Orthodox

Christians believe that at every baptism man literally and deliberately "*puts on Christ.*" Whether baptism comes about through the baptized person's own will or, as in the case of infants and children, through the will of the child's parents, this extraordinary and "impossible" mystical fusion continues to this day to take place regularly, as it has ever done, as the most basic rite in Christianity.

Moreover, St. Paul, after speaking of "*the mystery which hath been hid from ages*" and emphasizing "*the riches of the glory of this mystery among the Gentiles,*" actually comes out and succinctly defines this mystery in three one-syllable words: "*Christ in you*" (Col 1:27). Thus, though "*putting on Christ in baptism*" is never spoken of or even reflected upon by most Christians as actually being something that demands that the order of nature be overcome, it is, in fact, the most basic reality of Christianity and precisely what Christians believe happens in baptism.

The true lover of Christ, of course, will be led by the Holy Spirit to strive to confirm within himself the fusion of his fallen nature with that divine nature of the Godhead, first granted him at baptism. Is he not, as we have observed, called upon to "*bring forth Christ*" as did the Godbirthgiver herself?

iii

St. Maximos the Confessor easily recognized that the great and hidden mystery referred to by St. Paul in writing to the Colossians was, indeed, the Incarnation. In that ineffable and incomprehensible union of the divine and the human in Jesus Christ was manifest, he says, the blessed destiny of the world. Indeed, even from before their creation, all things, he says, were constituted by God for the Incarnation, since the Fall was foreseen, and the mystery of the redemption of the race in Christ was anticipated in that great mystery of the "*Lamb slain from the foundation of the world*" (Rev 13:8), referred to by St. John the Theologian in the Apocalypse.

Therefore, the Incarnation of God in Jesus Christ may be said to be the cause of all things, even though it was in no way at all, in itself, caused by any of them, St. Maximos insists. It was, however, with the Incarnation in view, he continues, that God brought into being the substances of all things. And this it is that constitutes the primary object of the divine foreknowledge according to which all things made by God were, indeed, to be recapitulated in Jesus Christ (Ep 1:10).

This great mystery, St. Maximos insists, does, indeed, enclose all the ages, showing forth the infinite great counsel of God. St. Maximos further argues that it even surpasses infinity, for it was eternally preexisting before all the ages. For all ages, as well as all things in them, were deliberated even prior to the ages. And they were, St. Maximos expounds, deliberated for Christ and in the mystery of Christ, whether it be of measure or measurelessness, of finiteness or of infinity, of the Creator or of creation, of stillness or of motion. It is this wondrous, mysterious union of all things from before the ages that was, indeed, finally revealed in Christ. Moreover, the Incarnation gave us not only the fulfillment of this revelation in Him, but also allows us to glimpse something of the foreknowledge of God.

It is, thus, only in coming to know Jesus Christ simultaneously both as the Logos of God and as the Son of the Virgin that one can begin to understand how we, as lowly creatures of God and belonging to the fallen race of Adam, actually fit into the "*mystery which hath been hid from* ages" revealed to us in the Theotokos. The holy Fathers speak of the "*dispensation*" under which the divine Logos, through his freely willed *kenosis*, deigned to empty Himself of His glory in order to take on the form of a servant, then to suffer and die for man.

In order for God to become man, however, He could no longer remain in the dispensation of the Godhead wherein He is forever and without interruption the eternally-begotten Son and Word of the Father. In becoming man, He, though immortal and the Creator of all things, also had to descend into a new, far less exalted dispensation, the dispensation of created being, the dispensation of mortality, embracing man's mortal state and suffering and dying and being buried as a mortal.

According to St. Gregory of Sinai, achieving a true understanding of the mystery of the two natures of Christ is of equal importance to achieving a true understanding of the mystery of the three Persons of the Holy Trinity. The combination of these two mysteries -- the two natures of Jesus Christ contained in one Person, and the three Persons of the Holy

Trinity, Father, Son and Holy Spirit -- constitutes, St. Gregory insists, "true Orthodoxy." Striving to attain something of that true understanding of those two basic mysteries of "true Orthodoxy" is, of course, the lifelong quest for every true lover of Christ. It is, moreover, something continuing until his very last breath, since in such an understanding of the divine mystery is to be found Life itself as revealed in Jesus Christ.

Indeed, in the Orthodox Church, "theology" always implies speaking of the Holy Trinity. In Orthodoxy, "theology" means speaking of God Himself, rather than peripheral church-related things such as, for example, "moral theology," "dogmatic theology" or "pastoral theology." It is for this reason that the Orthodox Church, unlike the Roman Catholic Church or the various Protestant churches, is extremely reticent in its use of the word "theology" as well as in its use of the word "theologian" when speaking of someone. The official title of "theologian," in the two millennia of Orthodox Church history, has been actually attributed to three saints alone: St. John the Evangelist, Theologian and Beloved Disciple, in the first century; St. Gregory Naziansus in the fourth century; and St. Simeon the New Theologian, who straddled the end of the 10th and the beginning of the 11th centuries. All three not only wrote ineffably of the divine workings of the Holy Trinity in regard to mortals, but they also demonstrated, through their lives, their experience of the implications of those deep mysteries.

iv

Just as the Incarnation of Jesus Christ resulted from the loving *kenosis* of the eternally-begotten Logos and Son of God, and came about that man might behold something of His eternal uncreated glory without being destroyed through encountering it, so too must man, in his fallen, incarnate state, move through a sort of reverse emptying out of himself. To be sure, this is certainly not an emptying out of the divine glory, for man has no glory apart from God. Rather, it is an emptying out of all that stands between himself and God. Thus only may he be filled with God.

Man is continually being called upon to respond to the descent of God offered him through the loving, divine self-emptying of the *kenosis* of the Logos in Jesus Christ. By Jesus Christ's accepting to be seen in a lesser glory and partake of man's human nature, man, by grace, is invited to become a partaker of the higher glory of the divine nature of the Logos Himself, thus fulfilling all that happened to him at his baptism.

Nonetheless, the dual nature of Jesus Christ does seem to pose a basic contradiction when we confront Christ's prayer in the garden of Gethsemane in the night in which He was betrayed. He, "*the Lamb slain from the foundation of the world,*" found Himself, as it were, praying to Himself to be spared the passion and death awaiting Him on the cross. How, then, was it possible that He, who is God and equal to the Father, would be praying -- even though "vainly," it turned out -- to be spared his Passion and death if he were indeed Himself truly God and "*the Lamb slain from the foundation of the world*"?

St. Hilary of Poitiers' observation about the two natures of Christ aids us greatly in grasping what these two natures are and enlightens us as to how they were simultaneously present in Him in His Incarnation. That great hierarch of Gaul, so rightly called the "Athanasius of the West" for his writings on the Holy Trinity, commented on St. Paul's referring to the "*God and Father of Jesus Christ*" by observing that in the dispensation of his Incarnation, through which Christ in his *kenosis* became a lowly servant, He, as a servant, would naturally call "God" Him, in the glory of Whom He was actually Himself God, yet, as God the Son, would also quite naturally address Him as "Father." Thus, because of his dual nature He legitimately addressed the Father both as "God" and as "Father."

Indeed, it is vital that Christians grasp that the human nature of Christ was, indeed, as we are taught in the holy Orthodox faith, a *perfect and complete* human nature, though without sin. Likewise, His divine nature was also *perfect and complete* in that He was Himself, indeed, God: the second Person of the Holy Trinity, "*by whom all things were made*" and "*of one essence with the Father.*"

But the startling challenge to the lover of Christ is to discover and accept that this *double* nature found in Jesus Christ's Incarnation is in no way to be limited to Him alone. Rather, it is to become a mark set upon all those who believe in Him and love Him. As the human race was drawn back to the will of God through the preaching the Apostles and their announcement of the saving mercies of God given the human race, Jesus

Christ was, indeed, announced as the new Adam of God's new creation, signaling a restoration of Paradise in man: "*For as in Adam all die, even so in Christ shall all be made alive*" (I Cor 15:22), St. Paul affirms.

The human mind, of course, is not used to stretching itself far enough to entertain such a possibility. How can something other than our poor, sad, fallen and created dispensation in which we actually exist be even possible? This explains why the ineluctable and totally unavoidable eruption caused in our lives by the mysterious dimension of death quite universally renders us uneasy. Be that as it may, a Christian, having been incorporated through baptism into the eternal dispensation of God, if he be a lover of Christ, will find himself having to confront the overcoming of the order of nature not just in the birth of Christ from the Theotokos, but also, by the grace of the Holy Spirit, through the ongoing process of the slow birth of Christ taking place in himself.

v

Be it St. John the Beloved, St. Paul or St. Peter, the holy Apostles writing in the New Testament all refer to how the great and mighty mysteries of the Christian faith were foreseen before creation, anticipating what was to be accomplished and carried out through the Incarnation of Jesus Christ at the time of Augustus Caesar. Their references to "*before the foundation of the world*" (Jn 17:24, I Pet 1:20, Eph 1:4) or "*from the foundation of the world*" (Rev 13:8) or "*from the ages*" (Col 1:26) all oblige us to take seriously the breadth, depth and height of the truly cosmic claims of basic Christianity.

From these basic claims Orthodoxy has never shied away. She has, indeed, ever proclaimed the two natures of Christ as firmly as she has insisted upon her own role as the Church of God and a sort of outpost of the Kingdom of the Holy Trinity on this planet.

It is both surprising and refreshing for non-Orthodox lovers of Christ to hear Jesus Christ referred to so constantly in Orthodoxy's liturgical texts as "*Christ our God*," as well as to hear so clearly reiterated Orthodoxy's fidelity to the basic teaching concerning His two natures. It is because of these two natures, moreover, that one sings in the *Canon of the*

Harrowing of Hell of how the image of each of us was actually already hidden in Adam. Though obscured even from the eyes of angels, our image was not hidden from Him, the eternal Logos, Who as Man was to suffer for every member of the human race.

Indeed, basic to the idea that Christ recapitulated all things in Himself is the idea that His two natures were, indeed, united in that one Person, the God-Man, who is Jesus Christ. One understands, therefore, why St. Paul speaks so boldly of Christ being all in all, and that it was no longer he, Paul, who lived, but rather Christ who lived in him. These are the words of a saint whose sanctity, he knows well, is not his own, but rather that sanctity given by the Holy Spirit alone, whereby the man who loves Christ is joined to Christ and, by grace, shares in Christ's glory. Did he not promise, through the Holy Spirit, that both He and the Father would take up their abode in the man who loved Him and kept His word?

vi

The revelation of the *"mystery which hath been hid from ages,"* however, is not a mystery revealed just by God alone, in the way the Old Law was revealed to Moses on Mt. Sinai, or in the way the Prophets revealed the will of God to the people of their times. This mystery was far too extensive in its implications, stretching far beyond the salvation of Israel as the "chosen people" of Abraham. The whole of the cosmos itself is implied and was to be affected by this revelation. Christ did not just die on the cross for the salvation of the human race on Good Friday. He also, St. Peter reminds us, in recapitulating the whole of creation and of the whole of the human race, even descended into Hades to preach to those who had languished there since Adam and Eve, awaiting the deliverance that only Christ can bring.

This new revelation of the *"mystery which hath been hid from the ages"* was thus inexplicably to be given man through the humble, almost unimaginable birth of Almighty God in a cave stable in Bethlehem from a virgin Mother in the form of a human baby born during the reign of Augustus Caesar. It was thus that God came to dwell with man in a new dispensation that was no longer a dispensation of the law, but rather a dispensation of intimacy, a dispensation of grace, for, indeed, *"grace and truth came by Jesus Christ"* (Jn 1:17). How far it was from the legalistic, fearsome dispensation of obedience to the Law given Moses, for it was the loving dispensation of joy given those who are the children of God and *"joint heirs with Christ"* (Rom 8:17).

Moreover, Orthodox Christians discover that it is in the most holy Theotokos that all the grace and freedom and joy of this new dispensation, granted in Jesus Christ, can be seen. In her is found, first and foremost, the liberation from law and from legalistic ways of thinking.

An Ethiopian story about the Theotokos beautifully illustrates the liberating grace flowing from her incessant intercessions for the human race and for the world. At the center of this story was what would be termed today a serial killer, a wretched, sinful man who had acquired an unnatural appetite for human flesh. He not only killed repeatedly, but always ate flesh taken from his victims. One day, desperately seeking to satisfy his passion, he spotted a helpless beggar. Though this beggar was also a leper, the sinful man's passion was so all-devouring that the man's disease did not put him off. As he raised his arm to slay the beggar, the unfortunate man besought him, in the name of the most holy Godbirthgiver, to spare him. Inexplicably touched by the plea of this rather unappetizing victim, the criminal granted him his prayer in the name of the holy Virgin.

When the serial killer died and appeared to be judged, his evil deeds were of such weight on the scales of good and evil that the Devil, seeing the scales tipping heavily on his side felt assured of his victory and exclaimed: *"He's mine!"* But the holy Virgin Mother of Christ spread her veil over the wretched sinner, claiming him for herself since he had, on that one occasion, shown mercy when asked for it in her name by that poor, wretched beggar.

vii

The new dispensation given by Christ is, of course, the dispensation wherein one discovers the mystery of the Church to be rooted in the mystery of the Holy Trinity, for the mystery of the Church is, indeed, the dispensation of the Holy Spirit at work in the world. That Holy Spirit poured out on the Day of Pentecost, 40 days after His Resurrection, at last fully revealed to man in the mystery of the Church what had been proclaimed at the Lord's baptism in the River Jordan: the Father's voice spoke to bear witness to the Son, and the Holy Spirit descended in the form of a dove and lighted upon Him.

This new dispensation was, moreover, also truly revealed to the race through the Theotokos herself, since, unlike her divine Son, she was not of two natures, human and divine, but of human nature alone, albeit a human nature "*full of grace.*" Still, as the role-model for all Christians who, like her, possess only human nature, she brought forth Christ and showed Him to the world.

It is not surprising then that, at Matins, the Orthodox priest addresses her as the "*Mother of the Light*" when he emerges from the Royal Doors, smoking censer in hand, just prior to the singing of her Canticle (Lk 1:46-54), known among Western Christians as the *Magnificat*, and serving as the basis for the Orthodox Canon's Ninth Ode. Indeed, she not only brought forth the Light of the World in Jesus Christ, but also continues to serve as a role-model for every Christian soul, male or female. She is also ever-luminous, teaching us to pray, as did she, before the most impossible eventuality, beginning with our own sanctification: "*Behold the handmaid of the Lord, be it unto me according to thy word!*" Understood as being in truth the Christian's role-model, the Theotokos implies that, in regard to man's relationship with God, there is, indeed, something quite other than the Western Christian idea of "imitating Christ."

The "imitation of Christ" has had a great vogue among heterodox Christians. Over the past five centuries, the little volume entitled *The Imitation of Christ* by Thomas à Kempis has proven itself a classic in Western Christian literature. *The Imitation of Christ* is, however, frequently viewed by the Orthodox with certain reservations as being far more "Western" than Orthodox in its orientation, as indeed it is.

In truth, what is taught by the Theotokos is not so much the necessity of "imitating" Christ -- that is, asking oneself what Jesus would do in such and such a situation -- but rather in allowing Christ Himself to take up His abode in us, as He once did in her. Cultivating one's inner life in Christ is the goal towards which one strives as a true lover of Christ. This is not at all found in trying to present what one is doing in the world as a sort copy of what one allows oneself to imagine Jesus Christ Himself might have done in a given situation. Rather is it to be found in something far, far more intimate and involving the whole person, not just the intellectual faculties of the imagination. Indeed, one is no longer relying on one's own reasonings, one's own feelings or one's own sentiments, but on the Holy Spirit alone. One is no longer striving to seek out an image of what Christ might have done, but rather to seek Christ Himself, that is the *being* of Christ, Christ's *living presence* in all its dynamism, that He may come and dwell in us through the Holy Spirit.

On this matter one has the Lord's own promise, after all. When the Lord was asked how it is that He will manifest Himself unto his disciples and not unto the world, He replied, "*If a man love me, he will keep my words and my Father will love him, and we will come unto him and make our abode with him*" (Jn 14:23). The key word here, of course, is "love": "*If a man love me.*"

And so it has ever been, as it was in the case of the Theotokos in whom He took up his abode and in whom the Holy Spirit continues to dwell as she continues in her cosmic role of interceding for all men. Is the great intimacy of the Theotokos with Him not the fruit of her great love, which, indeed, did draw the Holy Spirit to her that she might bring forth God from her flesh? Nor is such great intimacy limited to her: she is our role-model and shows us how to learn to bring Him forth. This is something that can never be the fruit of rules and laws, but rather of the grace of God. This grace is discovered in man's humble, unceasing prayer to God, as also in his participation in the Sacraments whereby he continues to fuse his flesh with the Spirit as was initially done in Holy Baptism.

The Holy Spirit was drawn to the purity of the desire of the repentant harlot, St. Mary of Egypt, to enter the Church of the Holy Sepulcher. Impure she may have been, but her desire was pure. Even in her great impurity, she desired nothing in that moment other than venerating the Cross of Christ as she was drawn to Him whose image she had put on in baptism but which had become obscured through her gross sins, probably committed only hours previous to this extraordinary experience. Drawn by the purity of her desire, the Holy Spirit came to her aid through the icon of the most holy Theotokos to whom she prayed, and she was immediately enabled to enter the church.

150

So it is that the purity of man's desire for God, and for God alone, by divine grace does allow the Holy Spirit to work in the most sinful man for his salvation in ways he is incapable of imagining. This seems a fairly common occurrence among the holy ones of God. Indeed, is it not accepted as quite normal that a saint's closeness to God is such that one actually recognizes and venerates the indwelling of God in such a lover of Christ? As He and His Father, by the Holy Spirit, both take up their abode in man, he, while not at all ceasing to be a man, can slowly be filled with the uncreated Light of the Holy Trinity.

In the discourse with His disciples when the Lord spoke not only of coming with the Father to abide in the man who loves Him and keeps His words, but also of the Holy Spirit, *"whom the Father will send in my name, he shall teach you all things"* (Jn 14:26), we find ourselves radically removed from man's trying to impose upon himself an imitation of Christ which he has spent hours thinking up as an appropriate demonstration to others of just how very close he really is to Christ.

Is it not inevitable that a person, in trying to imitate Christ, will find himself preoccupied with an "audience," that is, with the effect his imitation is going to have on those around him? How can one not be asking if his imitation of Christ is really sufficiently edifying? Yet, the true goal of one's life in Christ is never that of just producing an edifying example for others, but rather of intimate, personal union with Christ Himself. The imitation of Christ easily risks becoming a form of action that is preferred over Him Who is Being Himself, for the Being of Christ is not something man is capable of thinking up or even imagining, even though, through the grace of the Holy Spirit, he is capable of experiencing that Being and becoming a partaker of that Being.

Orthodox Christian living is neither an act that one stages, nor a theatrical production, whatever it may be with the complex demands sometimes made by Orthodox liturgical worship! Rather, Orthodox living is something inspired by the Spirit of God to which there ever clings the freshness of the Spirit's breath. Orthodox living is characterized always by a complete spontaneity enlightened by and submitted to the most rigorous respect for Christian tradition. This is something that Orthodox missionaries to this day are being called upon to demonstrate as they, moved by the Spirit, attempt to present Christ in unusual situations for which no one could prepare them and yet where they know Christ has led them. Learning to rely upon His abiding in them, with only the Holy Spirit to guide them into all truth, is essential. How much less rigorous Orthodoxy's more bulldogish zealots would all have to become were they daily challenged by the establishment of Orthodox missions in new, non-Orthodox territories! Yet, such has ever been the apostolic tradition presiding over the spread of our holy Orthodox faith worldwide.

viii

Non-Orthodox Christians, particularly Protestants, often express extreme uneasiness before the incessant and inescapable emphasis on the Theotokos in all Orthodox worship. One of the most striking of these is the priest's closing declamatory petition at Vespers, *"Most holy Theotokos, save us!"* Wanting to make their point that salvation can be found nowhere other than in Christ, Protestants often feel that such a cry sounds blasphemous and is basically anti-Christian. They thus accuse the Orthodox, quite wrongfully, of "worshipping" Mary rather than God, as well as of "praying to Mary rather than to God." With such basic arguments to counter, it is no wonder that the Orthodox often never get around to explaining the more spiritual side of what is really at stake in Orthodoxy's uncompromising, very deep and ongoing intimate bonds with the most holy Godbirthgiver.

Becoming an Orthodox Christian is, in fact, the true completion and the veritable fulfillment of every baptized person's allegiance to Christ, for at last one is incorporated into the whole of Christian history. One loses the highly questionable "advantage" of picking and choosing only that part of history which is edifying, just as in being a citizen of a country, the whole of the country's history -- not only the virtues, but also the sins -- become part of one's own personal history.

As the ever-virgin Godbirthgiver has, in Christian history, not ceased from the beginning to play an ongoing role, beginning with her *"barely prayable prayer"* of the one Annunciation, and continuing with her praying presence with the Holy Apostles as they awaited the descent of the

Holy Spirit at Jerusalem, the Orthodox Church guards a living memory of her interventions throughout Orthodox history.

Yet, as we have seen from the first chapter in referring to the liturgical rules of Orthodoxy, never is even the greatest feast of the Godbirthgiver allowed to replace certain basic required texts honoring the Lord's Resurrection each weekend. The demonic seems to encourage Protestants, who may constantly be asking others to pray for them, to reject categorically that power that 2,000 years of Christian experience have proven to the Orthodox is truly exercised by the most holy Theotokos as the *"Protectress of Christians."* Orthodox experience continues to teach the faithful that she is, indeed, the Christian's *"most constant mediation unto the Creator."*

The Protestant stance is derived from the demonic illusion that there is separation between those who are in Christ. Even though Christ did conquer death, death is still viewed by such non-Orthodox Christians as powerful enough to separate us from those who are no longer in this world, whether or not they are in Christ. It is essentially a tragic view and one bereft of the certainty afforded Orthodox Christians in proclaiming *"Christ is risen!"*

This is, yet again, a tragic fruit of Renaissance humanism, wherein man tends to replace God as the most significant thing in life, and whereby the human race has been radically severed from the intimate, ongoing dynamism of the Holy Spirit in the lover of Christ. Through this Spirit dwelling in the loving believer alone does the mystery of the Incarnation of Jesus Christ actually continue to be manifested through the faithful.

Since Orthodoxy never suffered the "Dark Ages" known in the West, classical learning and the Greek language both being part and parcel of who the Orthodox were, Orthodoxy also never experienced a "Renaissance" with its resulting humanism. The tendency to be radically cut off from God and from the workings of God's life in the faithful through the Holy Spirit is, in fact, far less severe among the Orthodox than among Western Christians where the whole culture continues to be marked and shaped by Renaissance humanism and its daughter, the 18th century Enlightenment. This humanist-Enlightenment agenda plays well with the singular and totally un-Christian goal of the man-centered Roman Papacy, declaring the Bishop of Rome "The Vicar of Christ" without which, the Papacy maintains, there can be no Church of God on earth.

The Western idea that God is very far away and can be seized only by the exercise of the believer's intellect, who thereby tries to bring Him nearer and apply His teaching to his earthly life, by a strange paradox can only eventually cut man off from the basic, Orthodox understanding that in Baptism one has truly "*put on Christ,*" and that, from that point, Christ actually lives within the believer through the Holy Spirit. It is this living, abiding presence of Christ within that must be cultivated and made manifest in the believer, through the work of the Holy Spirit; this is something that is fostered by the believer's own loving cooperation with that Spirit through unceasing prayer and participation in the Sacraments.

Just as the Incarnation was the fruit of the Holy Spirit's visitation to the most holy Theotokos, thereby gaining her sublime and eternal assent, so too does the believer, having assented to putting on Christ, also accomplish what was announced to him through his vocation to "*put on Christ*" by daily giving his ongoing assent. For such a lover of Christ, a constant, daily, even minute-by-minute offering up of his ongoing, loving cooperation with the Holy Spirit is essential as he strives to bring forth Christ from his flesh.

The ongoing nature of his conscious assent, as also of his cooperation, cannot be too strongly emphasized. Christianity is never a fixed, take-it-or-leave-it proposition, but a divine life in which one is invited to participate in complete freedom until one's last breath. How very far such an approach takes us from the fundamentalist (and, as with all things Western, highly conceptual) approach expressed by the familiar question: "Brother, are you saved?"

The mystery of the God-Man and His very intimate relationship with the race of men can, thus, bit by bit, gradually come to be understood by the lover of Christ, just as it was forever incarnate for us in the person of the most holy Theotokos. She, unlike Christ Himself, was of human nature only, a nature that she shares with all of us belonging to the race of men. Yet, in the new Adam that is Christ, God willed that the fallen race of Adam be restored to grace and to participation in the Paradise of His creation.

This eventual outcome of creation was, indeed, "*the mystery which hath been hid from ages*" of which St. Paul speaks that was revealed in the Theotokos. She bore Him, the eternal Logos, Who not only created all things, but Who came to redeem by His blood what He had created, sanctifying it through the Holy Spirit and raising it to the glory of the Father where He himself dwells with the Father and the Holy Spirit.

He is, indeed, in unconfused union, both God and Man. He was, indeed, born as a babe by the most holy Theotokos, manifesting thereby what was the will of God from the beginning, from "*the foundation of the world.*" Happy is the man who is blessed to catch a glimpse of this vision. Such a man can spiritually join himself to the elders in the beloved John's Revelation, casting himself with them before the throne of the Lamb, proclaiming unceasingly: "*Worthy is the Lamb that was slain to receive power, and riches, and strength, and honor, and glory and blessing!* " (Rev 5:12) Indeed, such a lover of Christ, as a member of the "*fellowship of His sufferings*" into which, by grace, he has, through the prayers of the saints, been deemed worthy to participate, may already, even in this life, join with all creation in joyously proclaiming before the throne of God: "*Blessing, and honors and glory and power by unto Him that sitteth upon the throne, and unto the Lamb for ever and ever!* " (Rev 5:13).

For a Christ-loving member of the "*suffering fellowship of Christ,*" there can never be a greater challenge offered him within the mystery of the church.

<u>Regina Orthodox Press</u>

A 40% discount is available for purchases of 5 items or more!

**For information, a catalogue
or to purchase books, CD's, videos,
tapes and other Orthodox materials
please call our toll free number listed
below or go to our website.**

Regina Orthodox Press
PO BOX 5288
Salisbury MA 01952

Toll-Free 800 636 2470
Non-USA 978 463 0730
FAX 978 462 5079

<u>www.reginaorthodoxpress.com</u>